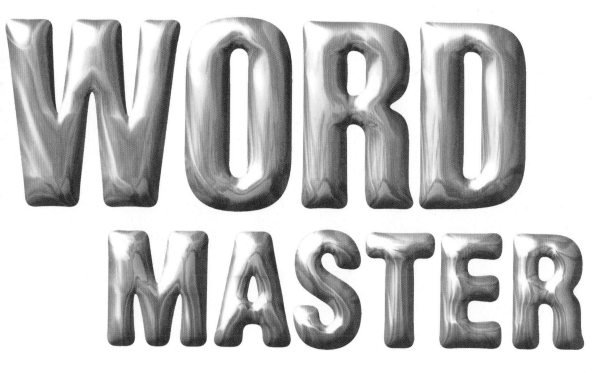

WORD MASTER

Sue Carrier

Letts Educational
Chiswick Centre
414 Chiswick High Road
London W4 5TF
Tel: 020 8996 3333
Fax: 020 8996 8390

First published 2004

Commissioned by Cassandra Birmingham

Editorial, cover and inside design and project
management by DP Press Ltd., Kent.

British Library Cataloguing in Publication
Data. A CIP record of this book is available
from the British Library.

ISBN 1843153289

Acknowledgements
The author and publisher are grateful to the
copyright holders for permission to use quoted
materials and images.
Screen shots reprinted by permission from
Microsoft Corporation.

Every effort has been made to obtain
permission for the use of copyright material.
The author and publisher will gladly receive
information enabling them to rectify any error
or omission in subsequent editions.

Letts Educational is a division of Granada
Learning, part of Granada plc.

CONTENTS

Getting started **4**

Copying and pasting **8**

Saving and opening a file **12**

Changing the appearance of text **16**

Aligning text and printing **20**

Setting up the page **24**

Spelling and grammar **28**

Finding and replacing text **32**

Adding bullet points and numbers **36**

Graphics and borders **40**

Adding clipart **44**

Adding photographs **48**

Text wrapping **52**

Columns **56**

Adding tables **60**

Working with tables **64**

Headers and footers **68**

Using text boxes **72**

Using word art **76**

Adding hyperlinks **80**

Adding sound **84**

Drawing **88**

Mail merge **92**

Index **96**

0101010101101010101001010101011101010110110000010101

SKILLS

.: Loading Microsoft® Word :.

In order to start using Word, you need to load the program and open a new document.

There are several ways to load a program. Here is one:

- Click with the left mouse button on the **Start** menu.
- Click on **All Programs**.
- Click once on **Microsoft® Word**.

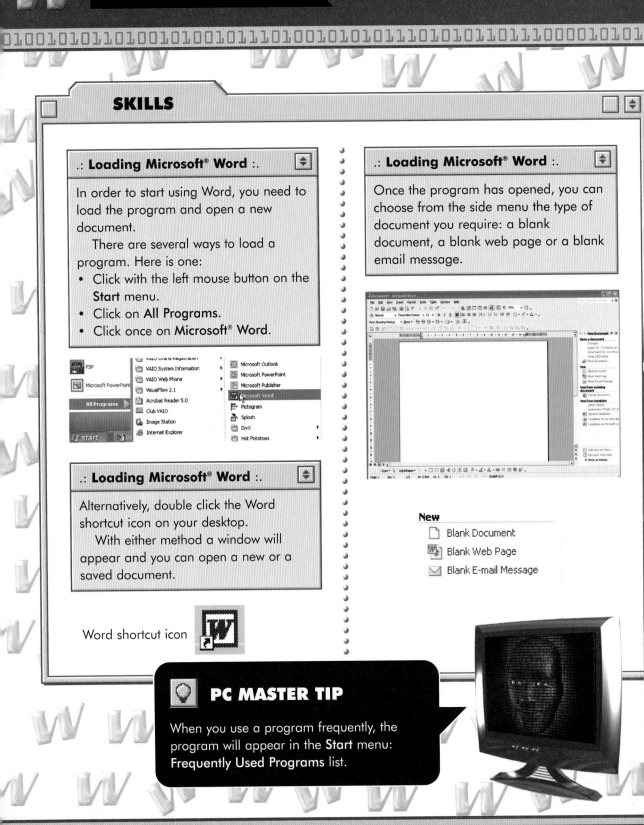

.: Loading Microsoft® Word :.

Once the program has opened, you can choose from the side menu the type of document you require: a blank document, a blank web page or a blank email message.

.: Loading Microsoft® Word :.

Alternatively, double click the Word shortcut icon on your desktop.

With either method a window will appear and you can open a new or a saved document.

New
- Blank Document
- Blank Web Page
- Blank E-mail Message

Word shortcut icon

PC MASTER TIP

When you use a program frequently, the program will appear in the **Start** menu: **Frequently Used Programs** list.

SKILL IN ACTION

Tammy the Teacher uses the word processor to prepare activity sheets for her pupils.

She opens a new document and types the text on the page remembering to use the shift key for capital letters.

If, as she is working, she misses out a word or decides to add more text she moves the mouse pointer to where she wants to add it and then clicks with the left mouse button. The pointer changes to a flashing cursor and she is able to add the additional text.

Investigating pop-up books

Look at the books your group have been given and answer the questions below. Make a short presentation to the rest of the class on your findings

Book 1

Title_____

Author_____

1. What is the back cover like?

2. Who do you think the book is for?

3. What genre is the book?

4. What is the book about?

5. What can you see on each double page?

6. What is the front cover like?

EXERCISE

Can you open a Word document and familiarise yourself with the following items on the page?

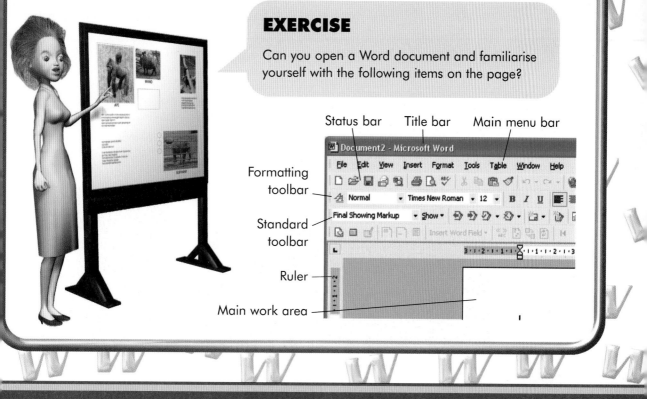

Status bar   Title bar   Main menu bar

Formatting toolbar

Standard toolbar

Ruler

Main work area

0100101011010010100101110100101010111010101101110000101 01

SKILLS

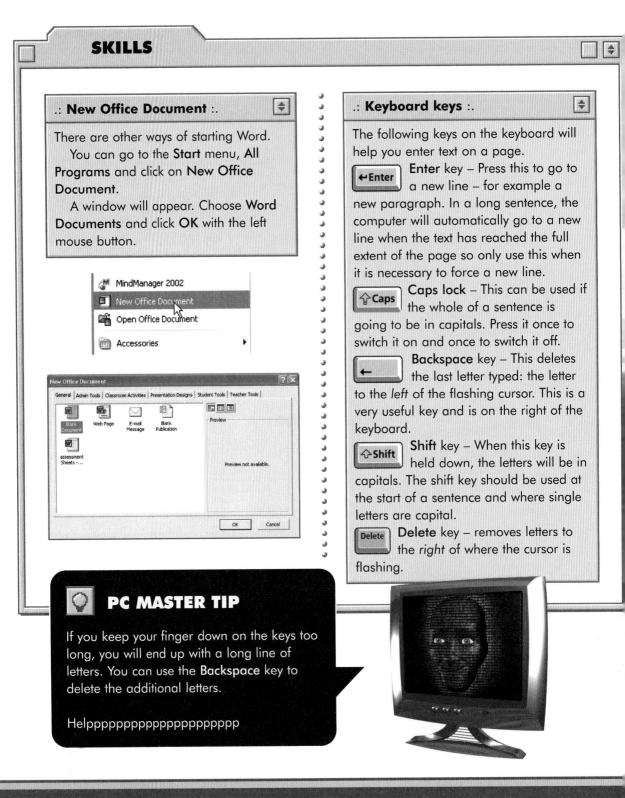

.: New Office Document :.

There are other ways of starting Word.

You can go to the **Start** menu, **All Programs** and click on **New Office Document**.

A window will appear. Choose **Word Documents** and click **OK** with the left mouse button.

.: Keyboard keys :.

The following keys on the keyboard will help you enter text on a page.

←Enter **Enter** key – Press this to go to a new line – for example a new paragraph. In a long sentence, the computer will automatically go to a new line when the text has reached the full extent of the page so only use this when it is necessary to force a new line.

⇧Caps **Caps lock** – This can be used if the whole of a sentence is going to be in capitals. Press it once to switch it on and once to switch it off.

← **Backspace** key – This deletes the last letter typed: the letter to the *left* of the flashing cursor. This is a very useful key and is on the right of the keyboard.

⇧Shift **Shift** key – When this key is held down, the letters will be in capitals. The shift key should be used at the start of a sentence and where single letters are capital.

Delete **Delete** key – removes letters to the *right* of where the cursor is flashing.

💡 PC MASTER TIP

If you keep your finger down on the keys too long, you will end up with a long line of letters. You can use the **Backspace** key to delete the additional letters.

Helpppppppppppppppppppppppp

01010010101101010010100101101001010101011101010110111000010101

PROGRESS CHECK EXERCISE

Can you open a Word document and type the following text?

There was an Old Man with a beard,

Who said, 'It is just as I feared!

Two Owls and a Hen,

Four Larks and a Wren,

Have all built their nests in my beard!'

Can you insert the heading 'Limerick' at the top of the text and the author 'Edward Lear' at the bottom?

Limerick

There was an Old Man with a beard,

Who said, 'It is just as I feared!

Two Owls and a Hen,

Four Larks and a Wren

Have all built their nests in my beard!'

BY

Edward Lear

Can you open a new document and type in the passage below?

When you have finished go back and edit the text by changing the words in red to describe an imaginary dinosaur.

Dinosaurs

Dinosaurs are vegetarians of the Jurassic period. They ate up to one ton of vegetation everyday. They would chew it slowly using stones they had swallowed to help them grind up the material in their stomachs.
We think crocodiles are descendents of the dinosaurs as they were both a dull green colour and frighteningly fierce. Dinosaurs came in many shapes and sizes but the most well known had a long slim neck and short legs.

MASTERCLASS

Can you write a short story and then edit the text by adding new adjectives?

SKILLS

.: Copy :.

It is useful to copy text and images to save time and avoid typing errors.

Select the information then click **Edit** on the main menu bar then **Copy**, or click the **copy** icon on the toolbar.

Copy icon

.: Locate :.

Click on the place that you want the information to appear.

.: Paste :.

On the menu bar click **Edit** then **Paste**, or click on the **paste** icon.

Paste icon

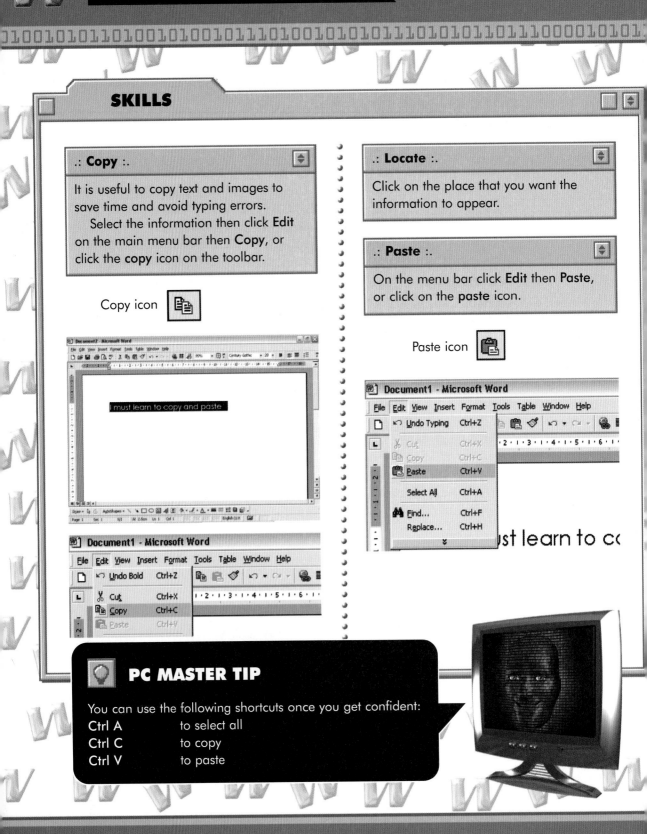

PC MASTER TIP

You can use the following shortcuts once you get confident:

Ctrl A	to select all
Ctrl C	to copy
Ctrl V	to paste

01010101010110100101001011101001010101011101010110111000101010

🗀 SKILL IN ACTION

Sophie the Student finds copying and pasting particularly useful when she wants to take text, images and numbers from a variety of places, edit them and turn them all into a new document. Remember that you must acknowledge any work you have used that belongs to other people. For example, if you were asked to produce a brochure advertising your favourite football team and you used a photograph that you had not taken yourself, you would have to say where you had got it from.

Come and watch the best football players in the world

On Sunday

14th September

At 2.00

Picture from Microsoft dipart

EXERCISE

Can you copy some text from a website and paste it into a new Word document? Read it, edit it and change its appearance before printing it out.

SKILLS

.: **Copying** :.

When copying an image from another document or a website, start by using the right mouse button to click on the picture. A menu will appear.

✂	Cu**t**
📋	**C**opy
📋	**P**aste
	E**d**it Picture
	Hide Picture Too**l**bar
	Borders and Shading...
	Caption...

.: **Copying** :.

Select **Copy**. Click on the page where you want to insert the image.

Right click again and select **Paste** or click on the **paste** icon on the toolbar. The image will appear on the page.

✂	Cu**t**
📋	**C**opy
📋	**P**aste
A	**F**ont...
≣¶	**P**aragraph...
≣	**B**ullets and **N**umbering...
🌐	**H**yperlink...
	S**y**nonyms ▶
	Select Text with Similar Formatting
	T**r**anslate

💡 **PC MASTER TIP**

When you right click on an image or page it always opens a drop down menu.

PROGRESS CHECK EXERCISE

Can you copy and paste text and images using different methods?

1. Open a Word document.

2. Type in the following text about William Shakespeare:

William Shakespeare was born in 1564, in Stratford-upon-Avon. Located in the centre of England, the town was an important river-crossing settlement and market centre. He was born on 23 April.

His father, John, trained as a glove-maker and married Mary Arden, the daughter of Robert Arden, a farmer from the nearby village of Wilmcote. John and Mary set up home in Henley Street, Stratford.

3. Insert a picture to illustrate the text.

4. Now copy and paste the text and picture using the Edit menu.

5. Copy and paste the same text and picture by using the right click on the mouse.

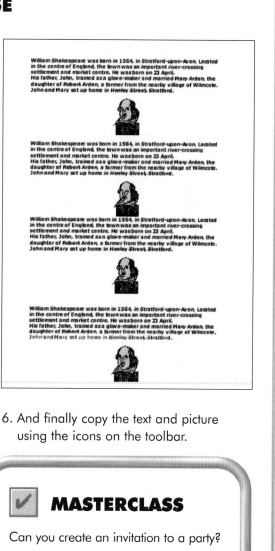

6. And finally copy the text and picture using the icons on the toolbar.

✔ MASTERCLASS

Can you create an invitation to a party?

Copy and paste it four times on one sheet of paper.

Save your work and print out the party invitations. (See pages 12–15 and page 22)

`0100101011010010100101011101010010101010101011010101011011000010101`

SKILLS

.: Edit and alter :.

Saving and opening files are essential skills. They allow you to edit and alter documents.

When you save a document for the first time you need to use **Save As** so that you give it a name.

Click on the **File** drop down menu and select **Save As**.

Give the document a name you will remember and click the **Save** button.

.: Saving :.

Once you have named your document you can resave it by either clicking on the **Save** icon

or by going to the **File** menu and selecting **Save** or finally by pressing **Ctrl** and **s** at the same time.

The name of your file will appear on the title bar of the document.

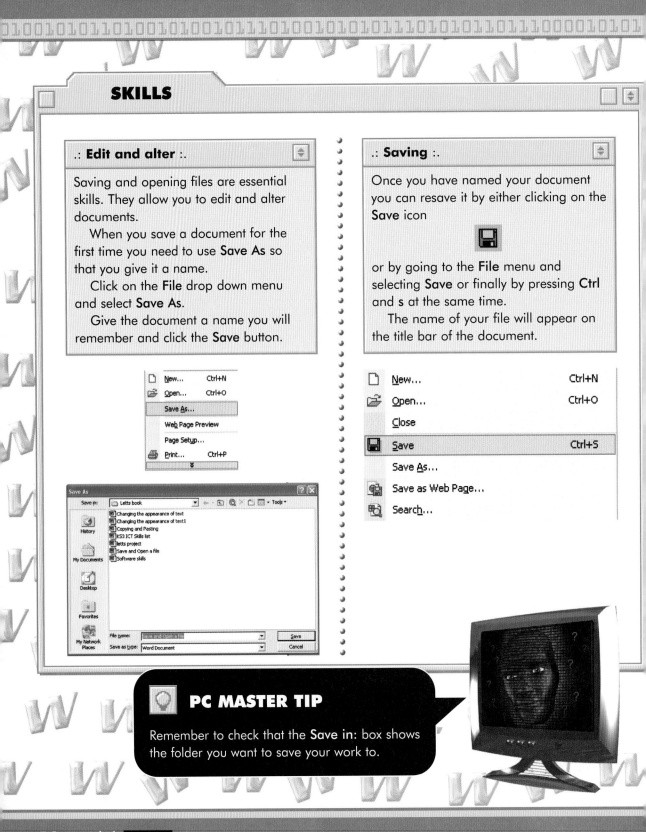

New...	Ctrl+N	
Open...	Ctrl+O	
Save As...		
Web Page Preview		
Page Setup...		
Print...	Ctrl+P	

Save As dialog box:
Save in: Letts book
- Changing the appearance of text
- Changing the appearance of text1
- Copying and Pasting
- KS3 ICT Skills list
- letts project
- Save and Open a file
- Software skills

History
My Documents
Desktop
Favorites
My Network Places

File name: Save and Open a file — Save
Save as type: Word Document — Cancel

New...	Ctrl+N	
Open...	Ctrl+O	
Close		
Save	Ctrl+S	
Save As...		
Save as Web Page...		
Search...		

PC MASTER TIP

Remember to check that the **Save in:** box shows the folder you want to save your work to.

001001010101101001001010111011010101011011000010100

SKILL IN ACTION

Sandy the Secretary saves time by using saved documents and editing them rather than starting again.

This is particularly useful if you are writing letters. You create the first draft letter and save it. Then when you want to send a similar letter, you just have to change the date, address and name.

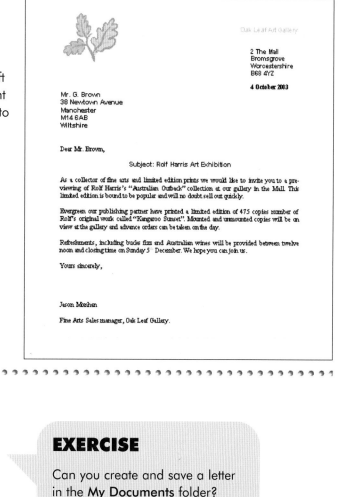

EXERCISE

Can you create and save a letter in the **My Documents** folder? Open it and make some changes, then save the new version under a different file name.

SKILLS

.: **Opening a saved file** :.

Click on the **File** drop down menu with the left mouse button and select **Open** or click on the icon:

Open icon

.: **Opening a saved file** :.

The window shown below will open. Click on the file you wish to open and click on **Open** with your left mouse button.

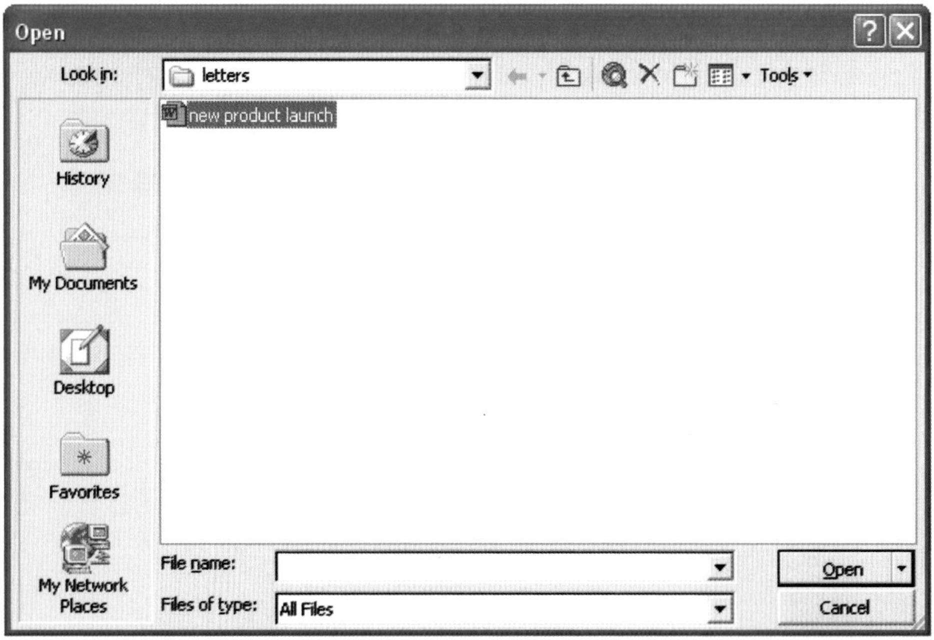

Open

Look in: letters

new product launch

History

My Documents

Desktop

Favorites

My Network Places

File name:

Files of type: All Files

Open

Cancel

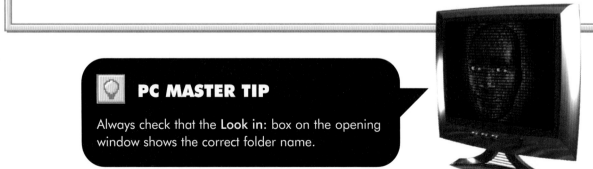

PC MASTER TIP

Always check that the **Look in:** box on the opening window shows the correct folder name.

PROGRESS CHECK EXERCISE

Can you write a letter to a friend?

1. Open a Word document.
2. Type your letter.
3. Save your letter.
4. Print your letter.

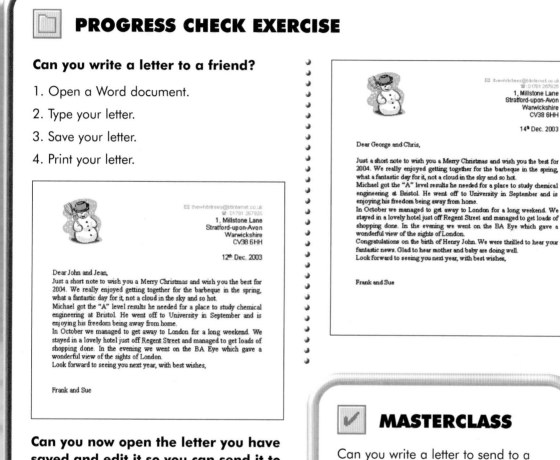

Can you now open the letter you have saved and edit it so you can send it to another friend?

1. Open an existing letter.
2. Make changes to the date and greeting line, and add some additional information.
3. Save your letter with a different name in **My Documents**.
4. Now save a back up copy to a floppy disk.
5. Print out your letter.

MASTERCLASS

Can you write a letter to send to a local councillor about the lack of parking in your area?

It should highlight the fact that it makes it very difficult for people who are trying to get to work, school and the local shops.

Draft a letter and save it as 'letter first draft'.

Open the letter and make some changes. Resave it as 'letter second draft'.

SKILLS

.: Selecting text :.

Changing the appearance of the text can add interest and emphasis to your document.

To change the appearance of the text you first have to **select** (highlight) the text to be changed

You can do this by clicking once with the left mouse button in front of the first word you want to change. Then press and hold the left mouse button down and drag the **insertion point** over the text to the end of the word or phrase. Release the left mouse button.

To do this: click once with the left mouse button in front of the first word you want to change. Then press and hold the left mouse button down and drag the **insertion point** over the text to the end of the word or phrase. Release the left mouse button

.: Bold, italic and underline :.

To add emphasis you can make the text bold, underlined or italic by clicking on the icons.

Bold — **B** *I* <u>U</u> — Underline
Italic

.: Changing case :.

To change the case first highlight the text. Click on the **Format** menu and choose **Change Case**. A separate menu will appear.

Choose the case you want and click **OK**.

Change Case [?][X]

- ○ Sentence case.
- ○ lowercase
- ○ UPPERCASE
- ● Title Case
- ○ tOGGLE cASE

[OK] [Cancel]

💡 PC MASTER TIP

Clicking once on the page places the cursor. Clicking twice on a word selects that word, and three times selects a block of type. To select a paragraph or more, drag the pointer down the left margin.

SKILL IN ACTION

Harry the Hotelier uses text effects on his menus in the following ways.

Font size can affect how easy it is for a piece of work to be read.

Text on a screen should be larger than that in a printed publication.

Larger font sizes add **emphasis**, e.g. headings and sub headings.

UPPER CASE WORDS ATTRACT ATTENTION BUT IF YOU USE THEM TOO MUCH, THEY ARE HARD TO READ.

Bold text can also add **emphasis** to single words.

EXERCISE

Can you make a menu card for a dinner party? Think about how you can use fonts, size of letters, and bold text to emphasise items on the menu.

Starters

Mushroom soup

Avocado and prawns

Paté and toast

Main course

Roast beef and Yorkshire pudding

Chicken in white wine sauce

Dessert

Crème Caramel

Death by Chocolate

SKILLS

.: Choosing a font :.

Select (highlight) the text to be changed. Choose a new font name from the drop down **font** menu on the toolbar. The menu shows you what the font looks like.

| Times New Roman | ▾ | 12 | ▾ | **B** | **U** | ≡ | ⋮≡ |

𝐓𝐓	Arial
𝐓	Comic Sans MS
𝐓𝐓	**Rockwell Extra Bold**
𝐓𝐓	Lucida Console
𝐓𝐓	**Impact**
𝐓𝐓	Verdana
𝐓𝐓	**Franklin Gothic Heavy**
𝐓𝐓	**Elephant**
𝐓𝐓	**Arial Black**
𝐓𝐓	**Eras Bold ITC**
𝐓𝐓	~~Accent SF~~
𝐓𝐓	**Accord Heavy SF**

.: Changing colour of text :.

To change the colour of the font, select the text to be changed. Go to the **font colour** symbol on the toolbar and click on the down arrow at the side of the box. Choose the colour you want and click once with the left mouse button.

Font colour icon

.: Serif and sans serif fonts :.

Serif fonts have small extensions to the ends of strokes – Times New Roman is a serif font.

Serif fonts make small text easier to read because they lead your eye to the next letter. They are used in newspapers but are sometimes considered old-fashioned.

Sans serif fonts have neat, straight ends to their strokes. They are used on websites, on screen presentations and are easier for an audience with impaired vision to read. This text is in a sans serif font.

💡 PC MASTER TIP

Using the **Format** menu on the menu bar allows you to change colour, font type, size, spacing and effects all at the same time. It also allows you to preview your changes before clicking **OK**.

PROGRESS CHECK EXERCISE

Can you type out a poem and use different text effects to add emphasis to part of it?

1. Open up Word and enter the following text:

The Eagle

He clasps the crag with crooked hands:

Close to the sun in lonely lands,

Ring'd with the azure world, he stands.

The wrinkled sea beneath him crawls:

He watches from his mountain walls,

And like a thunderbolt he falls.

Alfred, Lord Tennyson

2. Make the title red and a larger font.

3. Change the font style of the body of the text to bold or italic.

4. Place the author's name in a different font type and colour.

5. Choose your favourite section of the poem and emphasise it using the information from the Skills in Action tips.

6. Save your work.

7. Print out a copy of your work and annotate it, explaining why each feature has been used and how it adds emphasis to the document.

The Eagle

He clasps the crag with crooked hands:
Close to the sun in lonely lands,
Ring'd with the azure world, he stands.

The wrinkled sea beneath him crawls:
He watches from his mountain walls,
And like a thunderbolt he falls

Alfred, Lord Tennyson

MASTERCLASS

Can you create a poster to advertise Harry's hotel and some business cards for him to hand out to his customers? Use your skills, knowledge and understanding of how to add emphasis to a document using different text effects.

SKILLS

.: Aligning text :.

When you enter text and graphics into a document, you can decide where you want it on the page to create a more professional-looking document.

To change the position of text on the page you should first select the text that you want to move.

Then look on the toolbar for the icons below and choose the position you want for your text.

Click on the icon with the left mouse button and the text will realign.

Range text left   Centre text   Range text right   Justify t e x t

This text is ranged left.

ROLF HARRIS – THE ARTIST

Rolf Harris' love of art began at Primary School where he decided he wanted to be 'an artist....AND a good one!'

At secondary school he had an inspirational art master who recognised his natural talent. After leaving school Rolf studied to become a teacher, but continued drawing and painting in his spare time.

On leaving Australia at the age of twenty two, Rolf moved to London for one year and he enrolled at the City and Guilds Art School in London, wanting to follow in his grandfather's footsteps and become a portrait painter.

Today he is famous for his art and has a television series 'Rolf on Art'.

This text is centred.

ROLF HARRIS – THE ARTIST

Rolf Harris' love of art began at Primary School where he decided he wanted to be 'an artist....AND a good one!'

At secondary school he had an inspirational art master who recognised his natural talent. After leaving school Rolf studied to become a teacher, but continued drawing and painting in his spare time.

On leaving Australia at the age of twenty two, Rolf moved to London for one year and he enrolled at the City and Guilds Art School in London, wanting to follow in his grandfather's footsteps and become a portrait painter.

Today he is famous for his art and has a television series 'Rolf on Art'.

.: Aligning text :.

To align lists and to indent single sentences you can use the tab key on the keyboard. If you are using the tab key for aligning text do not use the space bar. Each press of the tab key moves the text a fixed amount. For example:

Artists	
Claude Oscar Monet	1840–1926
Pierre Auguste Renoir	1841–1919
Edgar Degas	1834–1917
Camille Pissarro	1830–1903

Tab key

PC MASTER TIP

It is better to type in all the text and then change the alignment. Then you can make other changes to the page appearance.

001001010110100101001011101001010101110101011011100001010

SKILL IN ACTION

Ahmed the Artist exhibits at art shows and presentation is very important so he uses different alignments on labels to create different effects.

Centred

This text always has the same amount of space on the left and right-hand sides. To centre text, select the text and click on the ☰ icon with the left mouse button.

This can be used for headings and posters.

Right aligned

This text lines up with the right-hand edge of the page and has an uneven edge on the left. To right align text, select the text and click with the left mouse button on ☰ the icon.

This is used for addresses and letter writing.

Left aligned

This text lines up with the left-hand edge of the page and has an uneven edge on the right. To left align text, select the text and click with the left mouse button on the ☰ icon.

This is the default setting and the alignment that is used most of the time.

Justified

Text is evenly spaced across the page so that it creates a straight line down both sides of the page. To justify text, select the text and click on the ☰ icon on the toolbar.

This is mostly used in formal documents.

EXERCISE

Can you create some address labels? Try different types of alignment to see what looks best.

SKILLS

.: Print Preview :.

Once you have created your document, you will need to print it.

Before you print it, you can preview it by clicking on the **Preview** icon or going to **File**, **Print Preview**.

Preview icon

Web Page Preview

Page Setup...

Print Preview

Print...   Ctrl+P

Send To   ▶

2 x 2 Pages

.: Print :.

In this view, you can see a single page or multiple pages. This allows you to see what the page will look like before you print it. While in this view you can make changes to the page layout using the alignment tools.

Once you are happy with your document, you can print it by pressing the **print** icon and it will print straight away. Alternatively, you can press **Ctrl P** and a window will appear. You need to check the correct printer is selected and then press **OK**.

Print		? X
Printer		
Name:	EPSON Stylus Photo 830 Series	Properties
Status:	Idle	Find Printer...
Type:	EPSON Stylus Photo 830 Series	
Where:	USB002	□ Print to file
Comment:		□ Manual duplex

Page range: ● All ○ Current page ○ Selection ○ Pages:

Enter page numbers and/or page ranges separated by commas. For example, 1,3,5–12

Copies: Number of copies: 1   □ Collate

Print what: Document showing markup
Print: All pages in range

Zoom: Pages per sheet: 1 page
Scale to paper size: No Scaling

Options...   OK   Cancel

💡 PC MASTER TIP

When in Print Preview, if you click on the **magnifier** button, you can edit the page in preview mode.

PROGRESS CHECK EXERCISE

Can you create a flyer to advertise an art exhibition?

1. Open a new page.

2. Add a heading to the page and centre it.

3. Include the date, times of the exhibition, venue and cost to get in.

4. Use the alignment tools to help you lay out your work.

5. Use the text tools to add emphasis and colour to your work.

6. Print preview the page and make any layout changes.

7. When you are happy with your work print it out.

Can you create a flyer to advertise a local event to post through doors?

1. Open a new page, type a heading and centre it.

Warwick at Christmas

2. Add this information:

Friday 5th December

Christmas Lights switch on

7pm

Warwick town centre

3. Use the alignment tools to give your flyer an attractive look.

4. Save your work and print it out.

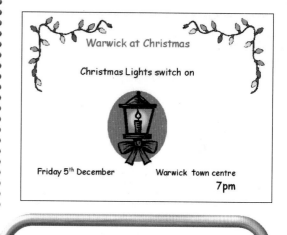

MASTERCLASS

Create a portfolio of your favourite pieces of artwork. Annotate the work by adding headings and additional comments and use the alignment tools to create the best effect on the pages. Preview your work and print it out.

SKILLS

.: Portrait or landscape :.

You can choose to set up your page landscape or portrait, depending on the task. This is known as the **orientation** of the page.

To do this, go to the **File** menu on the main menu bar and select **Page Setup**.

.: Page Setup :.

A window will open. Click on the **Margins** tab and choose either **Portrait** or **Landscape**. Click **OK**.

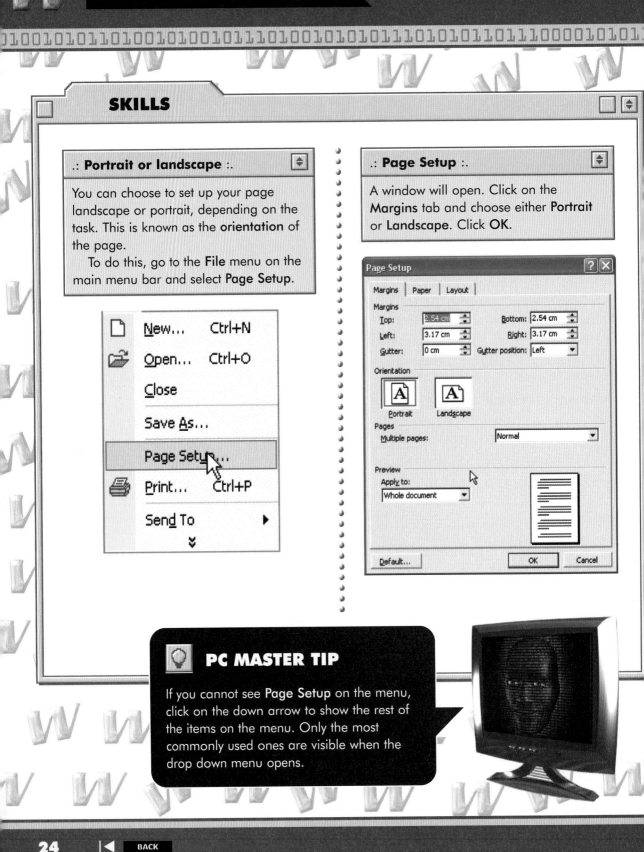

PC MASTER TIP

If you cannot see **Page Setup** on the menu, click on the down arrow to show the rest of the items on the menu. Only the most commonly used ones are visible when the drop down menu opens.

00100101011010010100101110100101010101110101011011100001010

 SKILL IN ACTION

Seema the Stylist uses Page Setup to allow her to create different designs for posters and leaflets in her salon.

This flyer is landscape.

Models Wanted

Don't miss this great chance to
have professional styling for
half price!

Seema's Styles

This poster is portrait.

EXERCISE

Can you design two leaflets, one landscape, and one portrait? Remember to adjust the design for each orientation.

SKILLS

.: Margins :.

Once you have decided on the orientation of the page, you can choose the size of the margins.

To change the size of the margins click on the **File** menu. Select **Page Setup**. A window will open. Choose the **Margins** tab. Use the arrow keys to change the margin sizes, depending on the effect you want.

The larger the margins, the smaller the working area on the page.

.: Gutter margins :.

A gutter margin setting adds extra space to the side or top margin of a document you plan to bind. It ensures that the binding does not obscure any text. To add gutter margins to a document, go to the **File** menu, click **Page Setup**, then click the **Margins** tab. In the **Gutter** box, add a number for the gutter margin. In the **Gutter position** box, click **Left** or **Top**. The preview window will show you the changes. When you are happy, click **OK**.

Koalas

Koalas aren't bears. The koala is related to the kangaroo and the wombat. The koala is a mammal. The koala bear looks like a teddy bear. The koala's scientific name is Phasclarctos cinereous.
Now there are only 2,000 to 8,000 koalas in the wild! Although not officially classified as endangered, the population of Australian koalas has dropped by 90% in less than a decade!
This is due to the destruction of the koala's natural habitat, a narrow crescent on the eastern coast of Australia. Logging, agriculture and urban development have not only reduced the area available to them, but added other dangers. The koala's habitat has been criss-crossed by roads, resulting in many road kills and attacks by neighbouring pet dogs are frequent. Disease, too, has taken its toll on the koala.

Koalas

Koalas aren't bears. The koala is related to the kangaroo and the wombat. The koala is a mammal. The koala bear looks like a teddy bear. The koala's scientific name is Phasclarctos cinereous.
Now there are only 2,000 to 8,000 koalas in the wild! Although not officially classified as endangered, the population of Australian koalas has dropped by 90% in less than a decade!
This is due to the destruction of the koala's natural habitat, a narrow crescent on the eastern coast of Australia. Logging, agriculture and urban development have not only reduced the area available to them, but added other dangers. The koala's habitat has been criss-crossed by roads, resulting in many road kills and attacks by neighbouring pet dogs are frequent. Disease, too, has taken its toll on the koala.

PC MASTER TIP

You can change the margin sizes by typing the size in the boxes in the **Page Setup** window.

PROGRESS CHECK EXERCISE

Can you design a page about your hobby using Page Setup to help you find the best layout?

1. Open a new page.

2. Change the orientation to landscape.

3. Make the right and left margin 1.5 cm.

4. Make the top margin 2cm and the bottom 2.5cm.

5. Insert some text about your hobby.

6. Now add an appropriate image to the page.

7. Make sure you format the text and images so they fill the page.

8. Now change the page set up to make all the margins bigger by 2cm.

What happens to your work? How does it change the appearance of the work? When might you use this layout?

Now change the orientation to portrait. Does this change the way your work looks?

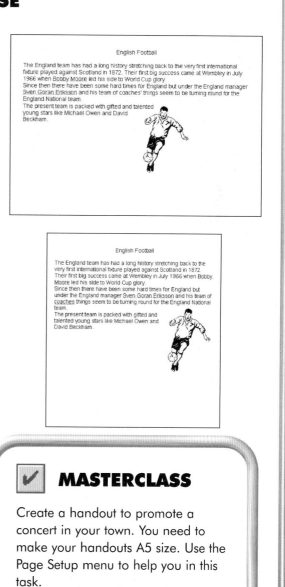

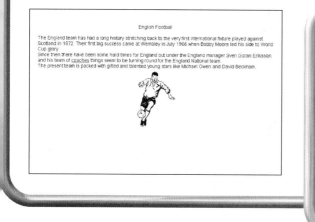

MASTERCLASS

Create a handout to promote a concert in your town. You need to make your handouts A5 size. Use the Page Setup menu to help you in this task.

Remember to make use of images and font effects for maximum impact and remember who your audience is.

SKILLS

.: Correcting text :.

Correcting text is a useful skill because it is easy to make errors as you type. When you enter text into a document you might notice that some words have a wavy red line under them.

This usually means that the word is either not in the Microsoft® dictionary or it has been spelt incorrectly.

■
The colurs that appear in a rainbow are violet, indigo, blue, green, yellow, orange and red

.: Individual words :.

Individual words can be corrected with the **Backspace** and **Delete** buttons (see page 6) if you know the correct spelling.

However, if you are not sure how to spell a word you can use the Microsoft® **spellchecker**.

Put the cursor anywhere in the incorrect word. Click the right-hand mouse button.

The colurs that appear in a rainbow are violet, indigo, blue, green, yellow, orange and red

.: Spellchecker :.

A pop-up menu appears.

You are given a choice of words to choose from. Select the one you want and left click on it. The word will be corrected and the red line will disappear.

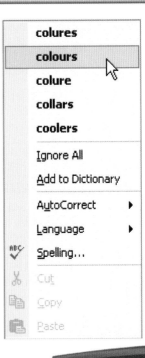

| colures |
| **colours** |
| colure |
| collars |
| coolers |
| Ignore All |
| Add to Dictionary |
| AutoCorrect ▶ |
| Language ▶ |
| Spelling... |
| Cut |
| Copy |
| Paste |

💡 PC MASTER TIP

Sometimes a word will be underlined but it is spelt correctly, for example a name like 'Michael'. This time, choose the **Ignore All** option from the pop-up menu. If it is a name you use a lot, choose **Add to Dictionary**.

0101001010110100101001011101001010101011101010111011100001010

SKILL IN ACTION

Donald the Doctor uses the spelling and grammar checker when writing referral letters and reports about his patients. The best way to work with a word processor is to get your thoughts and ideas down on paper. Then use the spelling and grammar checker to work through the document, ensuring that it makes sense and has no errors in it.

Healthy District Hospital
Sandy Lane
Morton
MO45 8HT

22 December 2003

Dr David
Get Better Clinic
58 Hospital Lane
Warwick
CV49 7BQ

Dear Dr David

Thank you for askin me to see this pleasant 76-year-old retyred gentleman. Today he complained of paine and stiffness, mainly in his left knee, although other joints were affected. He told me that the pain is worse last thing in the evening and during movment, but that there is residual pain when hee rests. He has been taking maximum paracetamol every day for the pain and is having trouble sleepin because of the discomfort.

Upon examination, the left knee is swollen and tender, especially over the lowe border. The range of movement is decreased in both left and right knees, move significantly on the left, and he he walks with a stick in his left hand.

X-rays taken today show losse of joint space and cysts consistant with a diagnosiss of Osteoarthritis. In light of these findings, I have prescribed him some stronger painkillers to take as required. I have disscussed the possable complications and outcomes of a total knee replacement with Mr Jones. He is prepared to go ehead with the operation, and therefore I have put him on my waiting list. He will be contacted directly about the operation.

I have discharged him from this clinic but pleese contact me if anything changes or there are any questions.

Your sincerely

Healthy District Hospital
Sandy Lane
Morton
MO45 8HT

22 December 2003

Dr David
Get Better Clinic
58 Hospital Lane
Warwick
CV49 7BQ

Dear Dr David

Thank you for asking me to see this pleasant 76-year-old retired gentleman. Today he complained of pain and stiffness, mainly in his left knee, although other joints were affected. He told me that the pain is worse last thing in the evening and during movement, but that there is residual pain when he rests. He has been taking maximum paracetamol every day for the pain and is having trouble sleeping because of the discomfort.

Upon examination, the left knee is swollen and tender, especially over the lower border. The range of movement is decreased in both left and right knees, move significantly on the left, and he walks with a stick in his left hand.

X-rays taken today show loss of joint space and cysts consistent with a diagnosis of Osteoarthritis. In light of these findings, I have prescribed him some stronger painkillers to take as required. I have discussed the possible complications and outcomes of a total knee replacement with Mr Jones. He is prepared to go ahead with the operation, and therefore I have put him on my waiting list. He will be contacted directly about the operation.

I have discharged him from this clinic but please contact me if anything changes or there are any questions.

Your sincerely

Dr Donald

EXERCISE

Can you type a letter accepting an appointment at the hospital? Use the spelling and grammar checker to ensure there are no mistakes in it.

SKILLS

.: Check whole documents :.

Rather than check individual words, you can check whole documents.

Click the cursor at the beginning of the document. Do not select any text. Then click the **Spelling and Grammar** button on the standard toolbar. A menu will appear.

Spelling and Grammar: English (U.K.)

fr	Ignore Once
	Ignore All
	Add to Dictionary

Suggestions:

fro	Change
fry	
far	Change All
for	
fir	AutoCorrect
fur	

Dictionary language: English (U.K.)

☐ Check grammar

Options... | Undo | Cancel

.: Spelling and grammar checker :.

To set up the spelling and grammar checker select **Option** on the **Tools** menu. Select the **Spelling and Grammar** tab. Decide on the options you want and select.

.: Spelling and grammar checker :.

In the **Writing style** box; select whether you want to check grammar and style, or grammar only. Click the settings.

In the **Grammar and Style options** box, select the options you want. Under **Grammar and Style**, select or clear the appropriate check boxes.

.: Highlights :.

Spelling errors are highlighted with a red wavy line beneath a word and grammar errors with a green wavy line. The spellchecker works through the whole document finding all the errors.

From Little Women by Louisa May Alcott

'Christmas won't be Christmas without any presents,' grumbled Jo, lying on the rug. Its so dreadful to be poor!' sighed Meg, looking down at her old dress.
I don't think its fair for some girls to have plenty of pretty things and other girls to have nothing at all, added little Amy, with an injusred sniff.
'We've got father and mother and each other,' said Beth contentendly, from her courner.
The fofur young faces on which the firelight shone brightened at the cheerful words, but darkened again as Jo said sadly, -
'We haven't got father, and shall not have him for a long time.' She didn't say' perhaps never,' but each silently added it, thinking of father far away, where the fighting was.

💡 PC MASTER TIP

The spellchecker will not correct words that are spelt correctly but are the wrong words for the sentence, e.g. Choose the Spelling option *form* the menu.

PROGRESS CHECK EXERCISE

Type out the poem as quickly as you can. Do not worry if you make mistakes: you can use the spelling and grammar checker when you have finished.

1. Open a blank Word document.

2. Type in the text.

3. Check the spelling and grammar to correct your work.

4. Save your work and print it.

Now type another article. Before you check it go to Tool options and switch the readability statistics on.

Now check your work. What do the readability statistics tell you?

The Walrus and the Carpenter

Lewis Carroll

(From *Through the Looking-Glass and What Alice Found There*, 1872)

The sun was shining on the sea,
Shining with all his might:
He did his very best to make
The billows smooth and bright–
And this was odd, because it was
The middle of the night.

The moon was shining sulkily,
Because she thought the sun
Had got no business to be there
After the day was done–
"It's very rude of him," she said,
"To come and spoil the fun!"

The sea was wet as wet could be,
The sands were dry as dry.
You could not see a cloud, because
No cloud was in the sky:
No birds were flying overhead–
There were no birds to fly.

The Walrus and the Carpenter
Were walking close at hand;
They wept like anything to see
Such quantities of sand:
"If this were only cleared away,"
They said, "it would be grand!"

✔ MASTERCLASS

Write an article for your local paper. Check it for spelling and grammar. Incorrect grammar will be underlined in green.

SKILLS

.: Find and replace :.

This is a useful function which saves time and effort if you need to replace a word in your document. It is particularly useful if you have written a very long document or if you have put an incorrect word in it all the way through.

You can find and replace by going to the **Edit** menu and selecting **Find**.

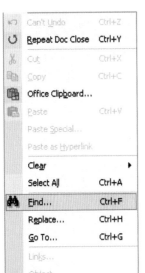

.: Find menu :.

Open the **Find** menu and enter the word or phrase you want to change in the box. It will find the first example of the word. You can then replace it with an alternative word.

Then click on **Find Next** and it will continue to search for examples of that word throughout your document.

.: Go To :.

If you want to check a page in a long document, select the **Go To** tab and type in the page number.

PC MASTER TIP

You can use **Ctrl F** to call up the **Find** menu as well.

SKILL IN ACTION

Tammy the Teacher prepares activities for her class in which they will use the find and replace function on the computer.

She gives them the sentences below:

- 'I don't like you', she said.
- The men said to the dog, 'Go home'.
- 'Did you find the book?' she said.
- 'Let's look for the others', he said.
- 'That's not fair', he said.
- 'Mending the car?', he said.
- 'Let's go to the shops tomorrow', she said.
- 'I really like going on holiday', she said.

Throughout the sentences Tammy has used the word 'said'. She wants her class to use the find and replace function to use more appropriate and exciting words than 'said'. This is one possible solution.

- 'I don't like you', she shouted.
- The men instructed the dog, 'Go home'.
- 'Did you find the book?' she queried.
- 'Let's look for the others', he whispered.
- 'That's not fair', he exclaimed.
- 'Mending the car?', he asked.
- 'Let's go to the shops tomorrow', she suggested.
- 'I really like going on holiday', she declared.

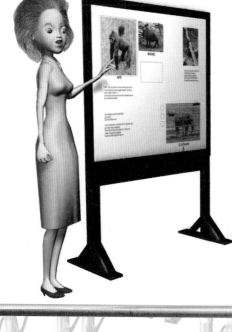

EXERCISE

Write an account of your last holiday. Use the word 'I' to begin every sentence. When you have finished the report, find and replace some of the words 'I' with alternative words such as 'we' or 'they'.

0100101011010010100101101001010101011010101101110000010101

SKILLS

.: Replace menu :.

Open the **Find** menu and select the second tab: **Replace**.

Enter the word or phrase you want to find in the first box. Then enter the word or phrase you want to replace it with in the second box. Click on the **Replace** button. It will find the first example of the word and replace it with the new word.

.: Replace All :.

Click on **Find Next** and it will continue.

You can click on the **Replace All** button. It will find and replace all the named words in the document.

.: Replace All :.

Click on the **More** button and you will get additional options. Search for a word, then click on the **Format** button. From this menu you can change the formatting of the word in a number of ways.

PC MASTER TIP

On the **Find** menu you can check the **Highlight** box so it highlights all the words it finds.

0010010101101001010010101110100101010101110101011011100001010

PROGRESS CHECK EXERCISE

Can you use the find and replace function to make this a more interesting story?

1. Type in the following passage.

Jack was very nice. He knew that the nice giant would be coming down to the nice village today. His nice parents had told him all about the nice giant.

   Jack decided to try and find the nice giant. First he found a nice rope which he tied to the nicest tree around. Then he collected some nice fish which he knew the nice giant loved to eat. After that he rang the nice bell to call the nice giant. After a few short minutes he heard a nice sound. It was the giant monster!

2. Use the find and replace function to change all the 'nice' words to more descriptive words.

Jack and the Giant

Jack was very handsome. He knew that the scary giant would be coming down to the quiet village today. His trusting parents had told him all about the frightening giant.
Jack decided to try and find the huge giant. First he found a strong rope which he tied to the largest tree around. Then he collected some fresh fish which he knew the scary giant loved to eat. After that he rang the loud bell to call the huge giant. After a few short minutes he heard a frightening and loud sound. It was the giant monster!

 MASTERCLASS

Write a document about your interests. Add impact to the document by changing all the key words to a different colour. Use the find and replace function to do this.

SKILLS

.: Bullet icon :.

Bullet points and numbers are used to make instructions and lists clear and easy to follow.

Before you start typing a list, click the bullet icon.

Bullet icon

.: Bulleted list :.

Type your list. Each time you press **Enter**, a new bullet will appear automatically on the next line. After you have typed the last item in the list, press **Enter** once more and then click the **bullet** icon again to turn it off.

- Bread
- Butter
- Milk
- Peanut butter
- Cheese
- Ham
- Chicken

.: Numbered list :.

To create a numbered list, click on the **number** icon and then type your list.

Number icon

.: Numbered list :.

Each time you press **Enter**, it will add the next number in the series.

1. Fill the kettle with water.
2. Plug it in and switch it on.
3. Put a teabag in the teapot.
4. When the water has boiled pour it into the teapot.
5. Place the lid on the teapot and leave to brew for 2–3 minutes.
6. The tea is now ready to drink.

When you have completed your list, press **Enter** once more and then click the **number** icon again.

PC MASTER TIP

You can add the bullets after typing a list. Select the items you want to bullet point and then press the **bullet** tool. If you want a number list, click the **number** tool instead.

SKILL IN ACTION

Sophie the Student uses bullet points in lists to help her organise her holiday.

Bullets add visual interest to a document. You can format the bullets and numbers to make them appropriate to your document.

Camping equipment
- Tent
- Sleeping bag
- Groundsheet
- Gas stove
- Pans

♥ Tent
♥ Sleeping bag
♥ Groundsheet
♥ Gas stove
♥ Pans
♥ Warm clothes
♥ Raincoat
♥ Hiking boots

Numbers can help you to decide on the importance of each task.

1. Shopping
2. Packing
3. Contact details
4. Visit relatives

EXERCISE

I am going to work in Greece over the summer with some friends. Can you write a bullet list of the items we need to take with us?

0100101011010010100101110100101010101110101011011100001010

SKILLS

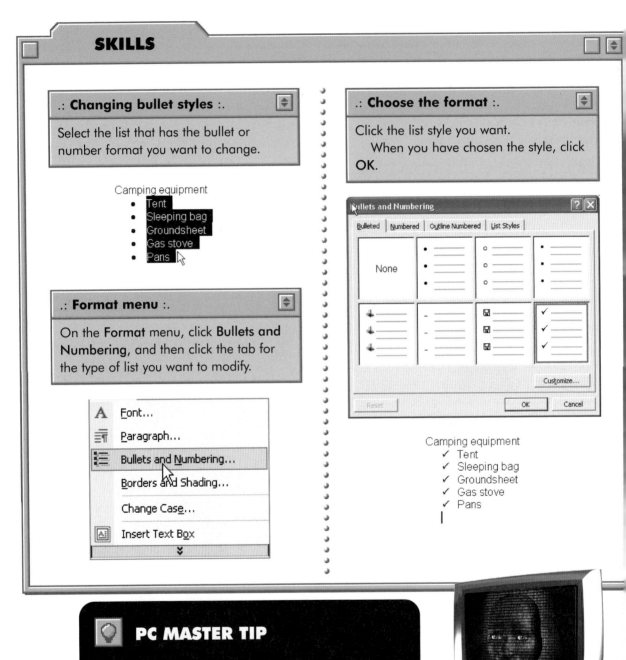

.: Changing bullet styles :.

Select the list that has the bullet or number format you want to change.

Camping equipment
- Tent
- Sleeping bag
- Groundsheet
- Gas stove
- Pans

.: Format menu :.

On the **Format** menu, click **Bullets and Numbering**, and then click the tab for the type of list you want to modify.

A Font...
≣¶ Paragraph...
≣ Bullets and Numbering...
   Borders and Shading...
   Change Case...
▣ Insert Text Box

.: Choose the format :.

Click the list style you want.
When you have chosen the style, click **OK**.

Bullets and Numbering

Bulleted | Numbered | Outline Numbered | List Styles

None

Customize...

Reset   OK   Cancel

Camping equipment
✓ Tent
✓ Sleeping bag
✓ Groundsheet
✓ Gas stove
✓ Pans

PC MASTER TIP

You can move an entire list to the left or the right. Click the first number in the list and drag it to a new location. The entire list moves as you drag, without changing the list appearance or numbering.

PROGRESS CHECK EXERCISE

Can you write out the recipe for pancakes using a numbered list for the method?

1. Open a blank document in Word.
2. Type out the recipe ingredients and method below.
3. Change the method into numbered stages so it is easy to follow.
4. Save your work and print it.

10 g plain flour, 1 egg beaten, 250 ml milk, oil, sugar, lemon juice

Work the egg into the flour. Slowly add the milk, beating until there is a smooth batter. Heat enough oil in a frying pan to cover the bottom and sides of the pan. Once the oil is hot, add a little of the pancake batter. Cook until the pancake is brown underneath and then toss the pancake so that it turns over. Cook the other side. When done, sprinkle the pancake with a little sugar and lemon to taste. Eat promptly.

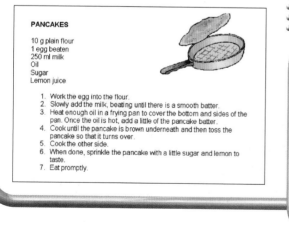

Can you now write a shopping list of ingredients you need to prepare your favourite recipes for a party? Add bullets to your list to make it easy to follow.

✔ 500 g carrots
✔ vegetable stock cubes
✔ bunch of fresh coriander
✔ 500 g cooked turkey meat
✔ 1 jar sweet pickles, chopped
✔ 1 jar mustard-mayonnaise blend
✔ 3/4 cup mayonnaise
✔ 1 pack devil's food cake mix
✔ 1 pack instant chocolate pudding mix
✔ 125 ml sour cream
✔ 1litre milk – semi-skimmed
✔ vegetable oil
✔ 4 eggs
✔ 125 g semi-sweet chocolate chips
✔ butter

MASTERCLASS

You are helping a friend write a cookery book to sell to raise money for local charities. Type out some recipes and present them in an appropriate way to make it easy for the reader to follow.

01001010110100101010010111010010101010110101011011000010101

SKILLS

.: Vector graphics :.

There are two different types of graphic that you can use in Microsoft® Word. Vector graphics are things like WordArt, AutoShapes and text boxes. These can be resized, scaled and stretched without distortion.

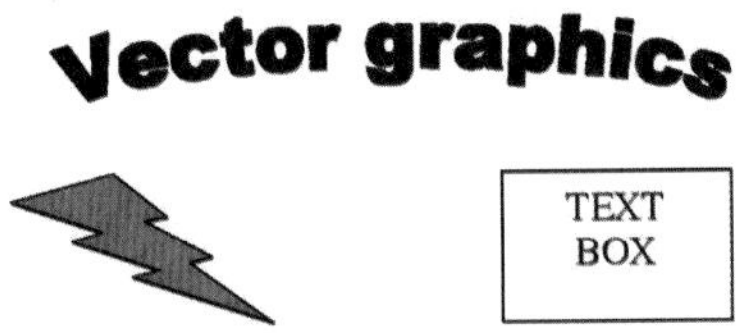

Vector graphics

TEXT BOX

.: Bitmap graphics :.

Bitmap graphics have file formats such as .bmp, .jpg, .gif and they include clipart and photographs. These can be created in painting packages such as Windows Paint. If you increase the size of these images you will get distortion and white spaces.

.: Inserting a border :.

Place the cursor on the page. Go to the **Format** menu and select **Borders and Shading**. When the Borders and Shading window opens select the **Page Border** tab. On the right of this window you preview the borders. By changing the style of the line, thickness or adding art you can create a wide variety of borders for your page.

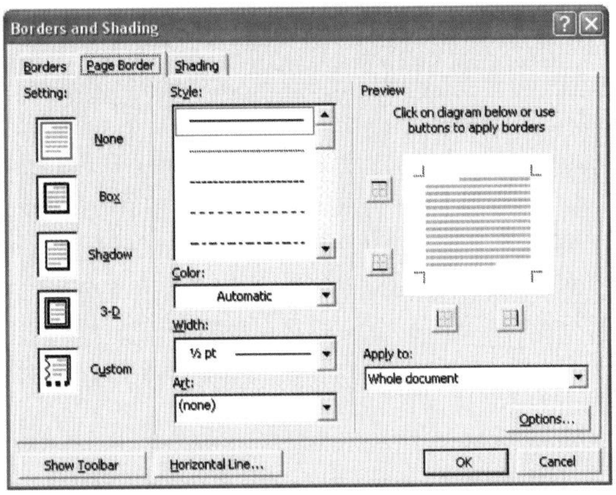

Borders and Shading		? X

Borders | Page Border | Shading

Setting:
None
Box
Shadow
3-D
Custom

Style:

Color: Automatic
Width: ½ pt
Art: (none)

Preview
Click on diagram below or use buttons to apply borders

Apply to: Whole document
Options...

Show Toolbar | Horizontal Line... | OK | Cancel

PC MASTER TIP

To move a graphic freely on the page select it then select **Format, Layout, In Front Of Text.**

0100101011010010100101110100101010111010101101100001010

 ## SKILL IN ACTION

Dave the Designer uses different types of graphics and borders all the time in his work. If he is designing a logo for a company he will use vector graphics and if he is designing a publication for a company he will often use borders and bitmap images.

To create a logo he uses a combination of WordArt, AutoShapes and clipart.

He then uses the logos he has designed combined with borders to create other publications for his clients, for example headed notepaper and web pages.

EXERCISE

Can you create a letter to a friend? Put a border around the heading and then pick out two other key points and put a border around them to draw attention to them.

01001010110100101001011101001010101110101011011100001010

SKILLS

.: Grouping objects :.

First insert the separate objects on to the page. Then, using the **Layout** menu, make them move freely on the page by selecting **In Front Of Text**.

Arrange the objects as you want them. Select all of them at the same time by selecting the first one, then holding down the shift key at the same time as selecting the others. Now go to the **Draw** menu and select **Group**. You can now move your new combined object all together. To make changes ungroup the arrangement. Select the object and click on **Ungroup** from the **Draw** menu.

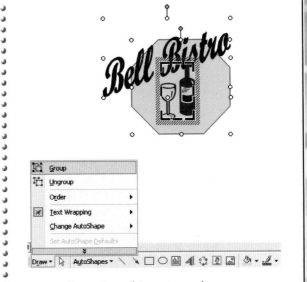

Grouping objects to make one.

Separate objects

Finished logo that can be moved freely as one image.

PC MASTER TIP

When all the objects are selected you can right click and select **Grouping, Group**. You can also nudge the object one pixel at a time by using the arrow keys. This allows for very small movements.

PROGRESS CHECK EXERCISE

Can you design and create a logo for a food product company?

1. Open a new Word document and insert an autoshape on to the page.

2. Fill the autoshape with colour and change the line style and thickness.

3. Create some word art for your new food product company then resize it to fit with your autoshape.

4. Choose a suitable picture from clipart for the company. Make it move freely on the page.

5. Arrange your objects together to create the logo.

6. When you are happy with your design, select them all and group them together to give you your finished logo.

7. Place your logo on the page in the top right-hand corner.

8. Add a border to the page to create some headed notepaper.

✔ MASTERCLASS

Use the logo you have created for the food company as part of the design for a web page. To get a blank web page select **File, New, Blank Web Page**. Now add your logo and other items for the web page design. Do not forget web pages usually have coloured backgrounds.

SKILLS

.: To insert an image :.

You can add pictures, scanned photographs or clipart to your documents to provide information and interest.

Click **Insert** on the main menu. Click **Picture** and then **Clip Art**.

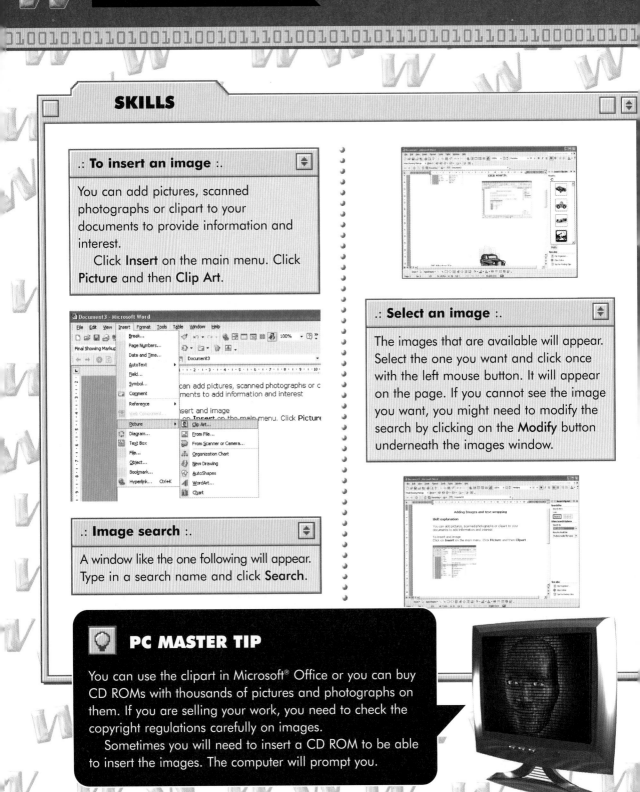

.: Image search :.

A window like the one following will appear. Type in a search name and click **Search**.

.: Select an image :.

The images that are available will appear. Select the one you want and click once with the left mouse button. It will appear on the page. If you cannot see the image you want, you might need to modify the search by clicking on the **Modify** button underneath the images window.

PC MASTER TIP

You can use the clipart in Microsoft® Office or you can buy CD ROMs with thousands of pictures and photographs on them. If you are selling your work, you need to check the copyright regulations carefully on images.

Sometimes you will need to insert a CD ROM to be able to insert the images. The computer will prompt you.

SKILL IN ACTION

Max the Marketing Executive chooses the type of image he uses for his presentations very carefully so it creates the correct impression.

Black and white images are easy to recognise and convey meaning clearly. They are good for signs and any documents that are going to be photocopied.

A photograph provides a more accurate image than a cartoon and gives a more serious feel to a document.

For example, in a holiday brochure you would probably use a photograph rather than a cartoon.

EXERCISE

Can you make a poster for your bedroom door to let people know that they should knock before entering?

1100101010110100101001011101001010101011101010110111000010101

SKILLS

.: Resizing :.

Once you have inserted an image into a document you need to resize it to fit the page and position it correctly.

To do this place the mouse pointer over the image and click once with the left mouse button. A box will appear around the image with little squares on it. These are called **handles**.

When handles are present the image is selected. If you click elsewhere on the page, the handles disappear.

.: Click and drag :.

When the graphic is selected move the pointer over the bottom right handle until it is shaped like a double-headed arrow.

Click the left mouse button and hold it down. The pointer changes to a single arrow. You can now drag inwards and upwards or downwards and outwards. A dotted rectangle will appear. This shows you the size the graphic will be when you release the mouse button.

💡 PC MASTER TIP

Always resize an image by using the corner handles if you want it to remain in proportion. Changing the size of the image by using the handles at the side distorts the image.

0010010101101001010010111010010101011101010110111000010 10

🗀 PROGRESS CHECK EXERCISE

Can you prepare an article on different types of transport and illustrate it with clipart? Resize the images to fit your layout.

1. Open a Word document.

2. Put a heading on the page: **Forms of transport**.

3. Insert three images of different forms of transport.

4. Position one picture in the centre of the page and write some information about it.

5. Add a second form of transport. Place this picture on the left-hand side of the page.

6. Add some text about this image.

7. Add a final image on the right-hand side and write about this form of transport.

8. Enlarge the image of your favourite form of transport to make it stand out on the page. Make sure you do not distort the image.

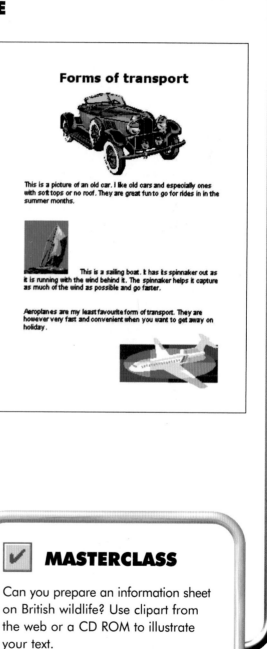

Forms of transport

This is a picture of an old car. I like old cars and especially ones with soft tops or no roof. They are great fun to go for rides in in the summer months.

This is a sailing boat. It has its spinnaker out as it is running with the wind behind it. The spinnaker helps it capture as much of the wind as possible and go faster.

Aeroplanes are my least favourite form of transport. They are however very fast and convenient when you want to get away on holiday.

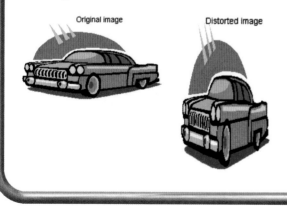

Original image   Distorted image

✔ MASTERCLASS

Can you prepare an information sheet on British wildlife? Use clipart from the web or a CD ROM to illustrate your text.

SKILLS

.: Adding photographs :.

When creating documents, you can get a more professional finish by adding photographs instead of clipart.

To add photographs and scanned images, you need to save them to a folder on your hard drive or a floppy disk first.

Go to **Insert** on the main menu bar. Click **Picture** from the drop down menu. Then click **From File**.

.: Select an image :.

A new window will open. Browse to the folder and file you want to insert.

You can see which folder you are looking at in the **Look in:** box.

Select the image from the ones shown in the window. Click on **Insert**. The photograph will appear on the page where the cursor was placed.

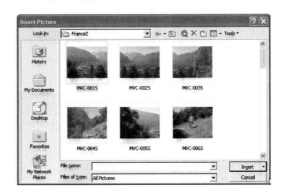

This is what you will see if you are in the correct folder.

PC MASTER TIP

There is a folder in **My Documents** called 'My Pictures' to save your files to. This way they are easy to find.

01010010101101001010101011101001010101011101010110111000010101

SKILL IN ACTION

Ahmed the Artist takes photographs of the work he does as well as that of the students at local schools where he works as an artist in residence. He wants to use these photographs to form the basis of his portfolio to show to employers and possible clients.

He then puts them into a Word document and annotates them so that when he goes for job interviews he is able to illustrate some of the projects and work he has done both on his own and also as part of the community.

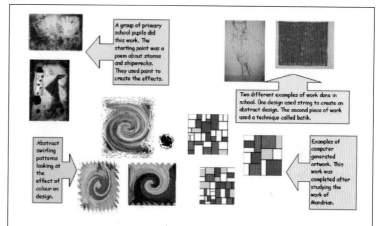

A group of primary school pupils did this work. The starting point was a poem about storms and shipwrecks. They used paint to create the effects.

Two different examples of work done in school. One design used string to create an abstract design. The second piece of work used a technique called batik.

Abstract swirling patterns looking at the effect of colour on design.

Examples of computer generated artwork. This work was completed after studying the work of Mondrian.

EXERCISE

Choose some photographs you have taken recently with a digital camera. Insert them on to a page and give them headings. Put a main title on the piece of work. Then save and print it.

1001010110100101001011101001010101011101010101101110000101011

SKILLS

.: Resize and position :.

To resize and position the image click once with the left mouse button on the picture. A box will appear around the image. Use the square handles to resize the image on the page.

Once the image is selected right click and select **Show Format Picture Toolbar** from the menu.

Using the **text wrapping** tool, position the image on the page.

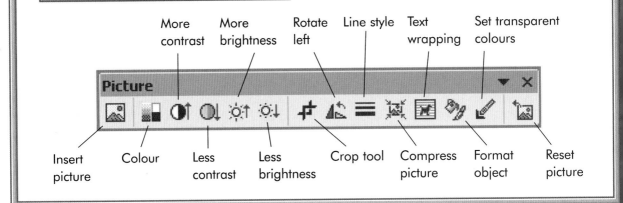

More contrast   More brightness   Rotate left   Line style   Text wrapping   Set transparent colours

Insert picture   Colour   Less contrast   Less brightness   Crop tool   Compress picture   Format object   Reset picture

💡 PC MASTER TIP

Before you include a photograph in a piece of work, put it into a program like Photo editor to balance and crop the image so it does not have too much background on it. This will also reduce the file size. Resizing an image in Word changes the way it looks on the page but does not make its file size smaller.

0010010101011010010100101110100101010101110101011011100001010

📁 PROGRESS CHECK EXERCISE

Australia

A koala bear hiding in a eucalyptus tree at the wildlife park near Cairns.

A view of Sydney Opera House from a boat in the harbour.

We went on a climbing tour to the top of Sydney Harbour Bridge. There were spectacular views from the top.

Can you insert three photographic images on to an A4 page and arrange them on the page for maximum effect?

1. Use the picture formatting tool to crop your images so there is not too much background.

2. Use the layout icon to allow the photographic images to move freely on the page.

3. When you are happy with the layout of the photographs add text to your work. Do not forget a heading for the page and some information about each image.

4. Save your work and print it out.

☑ MASTERCLASS

Send an attachment of some photographs to a friend by email. Choose two photographs. Put them into Word. Crop and resize them. Now save your document.

SKILLS

.: Format Picture :.

When you put an image on the page, you might sometimes want to have the text next to the picture or alongside it. To do this, you need to wrap the text around the picture.

First, add your text to the page and then insert a picture to go with it.

Red-eyed tree frogs have bright red eyes and are a really vivid shade of green with blue and yellow striped sides. They also have funny-looking orange toes. These are definitely one of the more beautiful species of frog!

Place the cursor over the picture and click the right mouse button.

A pop-up menu appears.

Select **Format Picture** from the menu.

A new window will open. Select the tab on the top of the page that is labelled **Layout**. You can now select the layout style for the picture.

When you have chosen the layout you want, click **OK**.

Cut
Copy
Paste
Edit Picture
Show Picture Toolbar
Grouping
Order
Set AutoShape Defaults
Format Picture...
Hyperlink...

Red-eyed tree frogs have bright red eyes and are a really vivid shade of green with blue and yellow striped sides. They also have funny-looking orange toes. These are definitely one of the more beautiful species of frog!

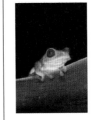

Red-eyed tree frogs have bright red eyes and are a really vivid shade of green with blue and yellow striped sides. They also have funny-looking orange toes. These are definitely one of the more beautiful species of frog!

💡 PC MASTER TIP

If you choose to put an image behind the text, make sure that the colour and size of the font are appropriate so the text does not get lost.

SKILL IN ACTION

Sue the Scientist has been creating information sheets about animals for a group of students who are researching rare breeds. She has wrapped the text around images for maximum effect.

The layout of the page is very important when presenting information.
Below are examples of different layout effects.

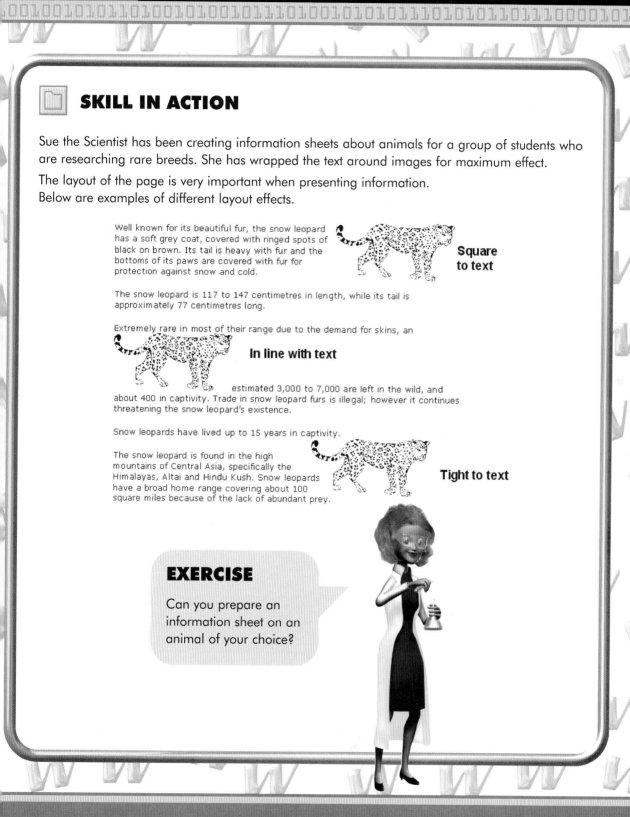

Well known for its beautiful fur, the snow leopard has a soft grey coat, covered with ringed spots of black on brown. Its tail is heavy with fur and the bottoms of its paws are covered with fur for protection against snow and cold.

Square to text

The snow leopard is 117 to 147 centimetres in length, while its tail is approximately 77 centimetres long.

Extremely rare in most of their range due to the demand for skins, an

In line with text

estimated 3,000 to 7,000 are left in the wild, and about 400 in captivity. Trade in snow leopard furs is illegal; however it continues threatening the snow leopard's existence.

Snow leopards have lived up to 15 years in captivity.

The snow leopard is found in the high mountains of Central Asia, specifically the Himalayas, Altai and Hindu Kush. Snow leopards have a broad home range covering about 100 square miles because of the lack of abundant prey.

Tight to text

EXERCISE

Can you prepare an information sheet on an animal of your choice?

1001010110100101001011101001010101011101010110110000010101

SKILLS

.: Square to text :.

To get the text to wrap around the image you need to do the following.

Right click on the image and from the pop-up menu select **Format Picture**.

Go to the **Layout** tab. This time, select **Square**. You can now move the image freely on the page.

As you move the image, the text will wrap around it.

Format Picture ? X

Colors and Lines | Size | **Layout** | Picture | Text Box | Web

Wrapping style

In line with text | Square | Tight | Behind text | In front of text

Horizontal alignment

○ Left　○ Center　○ Right　● Other

Advanced...

OK　Cancel

The Hare and the Tortoise – Aesop's Fables
Once there was a Hare who used to laugh scornfully at a Tortoise because he plodded along so slowly. "You never can get anywhere with those short legs of yours. Look at my long legs! They're so swift no one would dare race me."
All the animals of field and forest were tired of hearing the Hare brag. One day the Tortoise said, "If we were to run a race, I'm sure I would beat you."
The animals were astonished and the Hare, bursting into loud laughter, cried, "What a joke! That slowpoke thinks he can beat me! Come on, Tortoise, why I can beat you before you are even half-started!"
"You'd better not be too sure," cautioned the Tortoise
All the big and little animals gathered to watch the race. At the signal the Hare leaped forward in a great bound and soon left the plodding Tortoise far behind him on the dusty road. Looking back, the Hare could not even see the Tortoise after a little while.
"Humm, I'm as good as won this race already," he thought, "There's really no reason to hurry." So, as the sun was very warm, he decided to rest a bit under a shady tree. Soon he was sound asleep.
Meantime, the Tortoise jogged steadily along on the hot, dusty road, ever so slowly, but surely, and soon he passed the Hare who was still peacefully sleeping.
Quietly the Tortoise plodded on nearing the goal. When the Hare finally woke up with a start, he saw the Tortoise just reaching the finish line far ahead and he could hear all the animals cheering the winner. Boastful and careless, the Hare had lost the race.
Moral of the story: Perseverance wins the race.

.: Behind text :.

If you want an image to appear through the text, you need to select **Behind text**. Then select the **Picture** tab and change the image to **Washout** so it appears like a watermark on the page.

The Lion and the Mouse – Brothers Grimm

One day a Lion lay asleep in the jungle. A tiny Mouse, running about in the grass and not noticing where he was going, ran over the Lion's head and down his nose.
The Lion awoke with a loud roar, and down came his paw over the little Mouse. The great beast was about to open his huge jaws to swallow the tiny creature when "Pardon me, O King, I beg of you," cried the frightened Mouse. "If you will only forgive me this time, I shall never forget your kindness. I meant no harm and I certainly didn't want to disturb Your Majesty. If you will spare my life, perhaps I may be able to do you a good turn, too,"
The Lion began to laugh. "How could a tiny creature like you ever do anything to help me?"
"Oh well," he shrugged, looking down at the frightened Mouse, "you're not so much of a meal anyway." He took his paw off the poor little prisoner and the Mouse quickly scampered away.
Some time after this, some hunters, trying to capture the Lion set up rope nets in the jungle, The Lion, who was hunting for some food, fell into the trap. He roared and thrashed about trying to free himself but with every move he made, the ropes bound him tighter.
The tiny Mouse, scurrying about far away, heard the Lion's roars. "That may be the very Lion who once freed me," he said, remembering his promise. And he ran to see whether he could help.
Discovering the sad state the Lion was in, the Mouse said to him, "Stop, stop! You must not roar. If you make so much noise, the hunters will come and capture you. I'll get you out of this trap." With his sharp little teeth the Mouse gnawed at the ropes until they broke. When the Lion had stepped out of the net and was free once more, the Mouse said, "Now, was I not right?"
"Thank you, good Mouse," said the Lion gently. "You did help me even though I am big and you are so little. I see now that kindness is always worth while."
Moral of the story: Even the strong sometimes need the friendship of the weak

💡 PC MASTER TIP

If you want the image to look like a watermark, choose **Behind text** from the **Format Picture** menu.

PROGRESS CHECK EXERCISE

Can you prepare an information sheet on an endangered species of animal using the text wrapping tool to integrate the images into the text?

1. Open a Word document.

2. Insert some text and two images on the page.

3. Use the Layout menu to arrange the images on the page, one on the left and one on the right.

4. Make sure the text is square to the images.

5. Save your work and print it.

White Tiger

White tigers are very rare and can only really be seen in zoos. There are somewhere between 30 -90 white tigers in the US today. White tigers are not a different species of tiger; they are just white-coloured Bengal tigers. They are not albino either; they have blue eyes, pink noses and creamy white fur with brown stripes. White tigers are rare because they only occur when two tigers mate and both are carrying the gene for white colouring. Males grow to be about 2.62 metres in length, while females grow to about 2.37 metres long. A tiger's tail alone is 1.2 metres long. Male tigers weigh anywhere from 209 – 298 kilos. Females weigh slightly less, between 110 and 180 kilos.

Can you prepare a leaflet with an image in the background as a watermark?

1. Open a blank page.

2. Insert some text on to the page.

3. Add a relevant image.

4. Use the Layout tab from the Format Picture menu to put the image behind the text.

5. Use the Picture tab from the Format Picture menu to make the image a washout.

6. Save your work and print it.

✓ MASTERCLASS

Insert text and an image on to the page. Right click and select **Format Picture** using the Format Picture toolbar. See how you can control the layout of your page using the advanced features of text wrapping. Click on the **Advanced** button. You can now choose whether the text goes to the right, left or to both sides of the image. You can also choose the distance the text is from the image. When you have made your choice, click **OK** and then **OK** again on the **Format Picture** screen.

1001010110100101001011101001010101011101010110111000010101

SKILLS

.: Columns :.

There are many uses for columns in Word. Newsletters, leaflets and newspapers are a few ideas. Columns allow you to present your work in a way that can be eye-catching.

Making columns in Word is easy. First of all you need to create the text you want to put into columns. When you have written it as a normal document, you change the presentation and put it into columns by clicking on the **columns** icon and choosing the number of columns needed.

Columns icon

2 Columns

Could watching television be bad for your health?

UK doctors are worried over the increasing numbers of people suffering from a new virus known as "telly belly". This is when people suffer from copycat illnesses after they've watched a health programme on television.

A new report shows that nine out of ten doctors believe that TV, radio and newspaper coverage of health problems affects patients.

More and more people are coming down with similar symptoms to those they see on television.

Increasingly people are self-diagnosing their problems. This means they use books and websites to find out what their symptoms might mean.

But this current trend means that people are seeing things on TV, and then thinking that they feel ill. They then put two and two together to diagnose themselves with what they've just seen their favourite soap star suffering from.

3 Columns

Could watching television be bad for your health?

UK doctors are worried over the increasing numbers of people suffering from a new virus known as "telly belly". This is when people suffer from copycat illnesses after they've watched a health programme on television.

A new report shows that nine out of ten doctors believe that TV, radio and newspaper coverage of health problems affects patients. More and more people are coming down with similar symptoms to those they see on television.

Increasingly people are self- diagnosing their problems. This means they use books and websites to find out what their symptoms might mean.

But this current trend means that people are seeing things on TV, and then thinking that they feel ill. They then put two and two together to diagnose themselves with what they've just seen their favourite soap star suffering from.

💡 PC MASTER TIP

Decide on the orientation of the page before you start working. Make sure the columns are not too narrow on the page.

001001010101101001010010101101001010101011101010110111000010101

SKILL IN ACTION

Nick the Newspaper Editor often uses columns in his paper. When he is preparing articles for the paper, he writes the article first.

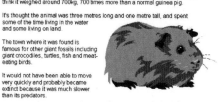

Giant Fossils

Scientists have found the fossil remains of the biggest rodent ever, an animal like a guinea pig the size of a buffalo. It would have lived on the earth more than eight million years ago.

The scientists found the fossils in the South American country Venezuela, and think it weighed around 700kg, 700 times more than a normal guinea pig.

It's thought the animal was three metres long and one metre tall, and spent some of the time living in the water and some living on land.

The town where it was found is famous for other giant fossils including giant crocodiles, turtles, fish and meat-eating birds.

It would not have been able to move very quickly and probably became extinct because it was much slower than its predators.

Then he decides how many columns he wants the story to be in and selects the number from the columns menu.

2 Columns

Sometimes Nick uses a mixture of columns and text that goes across the whole page. He does this for effect or to get the maximum amount of information on a page.

Giant Fossils

Scientists have found the fossil remains of the biggest rodent ever, an animal like a guinea pig the size of a buffalo. It would have lived on the earth more than eight million years ago.

The scientists found the fossils in the South American country Venezuela, and think it weighed around 700kg, 700 times more than a normal guinea pig.

It's thought the animal was three metres long and one metre tall, and spent some of the time living in the water and some living on land.

The town where it was found is famous for other giant fossils including giant crocodiles, turtles, fish and meat-eating birds.

It would not have been able to move very quickly and probably became extinct because it was much slower than its predators.

Giant Fossils

Scientists have found the fossil remains of the biggest rodent ever, an animal like a guinea pig the size of a buffalo. It would have lived on the earth more than eight million years ago.

The scientists found the fossils in the South American country Venezuela, and think it weighed around 700kg, 700 times more than a normal guinea pig.

It's thought the animal was three metres long and one metre tall, and spent some of the time living in the water and some living on land.

The town where it was found is famous for other giant fossils including giant crocodiles, turtles, fish and meat-eating birds.

It would not have been able to move very quickly and probably became extinct because it was much slower than its predators.

EXERCISE

Write a story for your local newspaper. Can you present it in two columns on a portrait page?

EDITOR

SKILLS

.: Formatting columns :.

Select the text you want to put into columns. Select **Columns** from **Format** on the menu bar. A window will open.

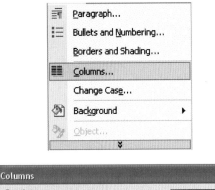

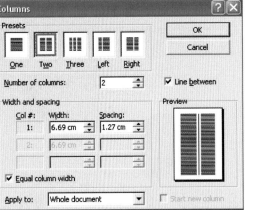

.: Formatting columns :.

Now you can decide on the number of columns and the width of the columns. You can also choose whether there is a line in between the columns and how much space there is between them. The **Preview** window shows you how the page layout will look. When you are happy with it, click **OK**.

Law change for junk e-mail

People who send junk e-mails could be fined £5,000 under new European laws which came into force on Thursday. Millions of junk e-mails - known as spam - are sent out every day. Spam makes up 50% of e-mail traffic. It clogs up inboxes, slows down the net and jams servers. Some of the content is really upsetting and inappropriate. A recent survey showed that spam is not overwhelming the inboxes of workers, despite the growing number of junk e-mails promoting get-rich-quick scams or pornographic websites. Instead junk e-mails seem to be more of a problem for personal accounts. The survey shows that e-mail plays an important part in keeping workers communicating with each other. Almost three-quarters

say it helps them communicate with more people, although a third says that e-mail makes them too accessible. Some people think the laws won't work because they only apply to Europe and most spam comes from the US. The fine has also been criticised as too low. What's more, spammers are really good at hiding their identity, so it will be hard to track them down and fine them.
Coping with spam
Even if the laws don't work, there are some things you can do to avoid spam. "Never open up what looks like a spam e-mail or virus e-mail, never forward it on to anyone else, never reply to it and be careful what you sign on to when you're online,"

PC MASTER TIP

Using the **Format** menu to create columns allows you to vary the width of the columns and put lines between them.

10100101011010010100101110100101010111010101101110000101010

PROGRESS CHECK EXERCISE

Can you make a news article for a teenage magazine?

1. Copy a piece of text from the internet on a subject that interests you.

2. Change the appearance of the text to make it more appealing to readers.

3. Using the columns tool, turn your article into a page from a newspaper or magazine.

4. Think about the layout of the page so that you get maximum interest and impact.

5. Add appropriate images.

6. Save your work.

7. Print off a copy and ask a friend whether they think you have produced an article suitable for a teenage magazine.

Teenagers 'Hate their Body image'

A recent survey showed that nine out of ten teenage girls are unhappy with their body. There were approximately 3000 girls questioned and only 8% of them where '**HAPPY**' with their appearance and over 50% where prepared to say they where '**UN HAPPY**' with the way they looked.

Out of the girls questioned only 20% where actually overweight but a massive 70% thought they ought to lose weight. Even more worrying was the fact that 60% of the girls questioned had been on a diet before they were 13. This problem is not one that just affects girls; a further study found almost half of girls and a third of boys aged between seven and twelve wanted to be thinner. Approximately a fifth said they were "already suffering from an eating disorder" such as anorexia or bulimia.

It was also found that boys with eating disorders could miss out on treatment because their illnesses are not being picked up by parents and doctors. This is because eating disorders like anorexia are much more common in girls and doctors and parents think some boys are shy about discussing their eating habits because they see them as girls' problems.

Another worrying statistic in the survey was that more than a quarter of 14-year-olds say they had considered having plastic surgery or taking diet pills. Scientists blame the body shapes of skinny celebs for putting this pressure on young people. From a selection of photographs, children were asked to pick out which image they thought was most like their own and which one they thought was an ideal figure. Scientists found that 60% of girls selected an ideal body image that was thinner than their own with 50% of boys preferring a thinner body image.

Why is looking good important to teenagers?

Some studies have shown that 'attractive' people often do better in society:

Attractive children are more popular and children believe teachers give them better grades.

It is thought that attractive applicants have a better chance of getting jobs, and of getting paid more.

In court, attractive people are found guilty less often. When found guilty, they receive less punishment.

All this make us feel that we have to have a perfect body image and is applying pressure on the teenagers of today.

MASTERCLASS

Prepare the front page of a newspaper. Use both text and images on the page. Think about the layout, font type and size that are going to create the maximum impact.

SKILLS

.: Table menu :.

Tables are very useful for organising information on a page. They keep lists in columns and rows.

To add a table to the page click on the **Table** menu on the menu bar. Select **Insert** from the drop down menu.

A window will open. Enter the number of columns and rows you want in your table.

To enter text in the table, just click in the boxes and type.

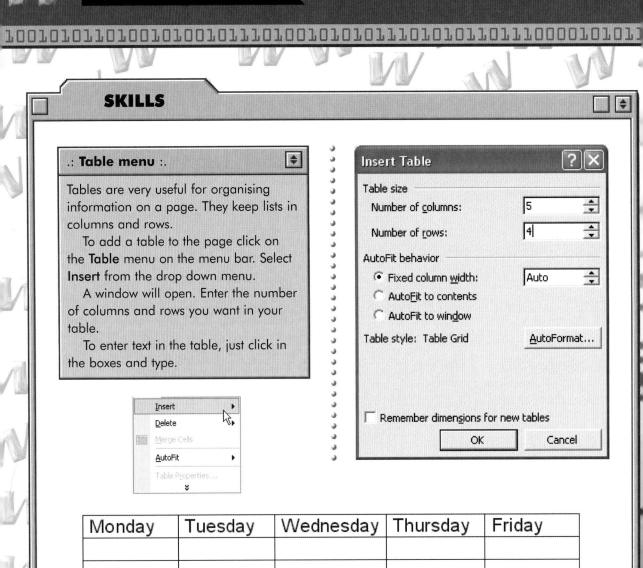

Insert Table

Table size
Number of columns: 5
Number of rows: 4

AutoFit behavior
● Fixed column width: Auto
○ AutoFit to contents
○ AutoFit to window

Table style: Table Grid   AutoFormat...

☐ Remember dimensions for new tables

OK   Cancel

Insert
Delete
Merge Cells
AutoFit
Table Properties...

Monday	Tuesday	Wednesday	Thursday	Friday

💡 PC MASTER TIP

The columns and rows will all be equally spaced. The computer will automatically fit the table inside the margins of the page.

01010010101011010010101001011101001010101011101010110110110000101010

 ## SKILL IN ACTION

Cassie the Cook uses tables to draw up a work rota for the kitchen every week. First she draws a table with six rows and five columns. She puts the days of the week down the side and the names of the staff along the top. She then indicates in each box if somebody is working or not.

Days of the week	Cassie	Jim	Susie	Frank
Monday	√		√	√
Tuesday		√	√	√
Wednesday	√	√	√	√
Thursday	√	√	√	
Friday	√	√		√

EXERCISE

I need to draw up a table to show when the staff are on holiday during August. Can you draw up a table for me and mark in the holiday dates?

Cassie is on holiday for 15 days.
Jim is away for a fortnight.
Susie is away for 10 days.
Frank is away for a week.
Ensure that there are always two staff on duty at any one time.

010010101101001010010111010010101010111010101101110000100101

SKILLS

.: Drawing a table :.

Sometimes it is easier to draw the table than insert it. To do this, you use the **draw table** tool.

This icon opens the **Tables and Borders** toolbar.

.: Choose style :.

Choose the line style and thickness from the drop down menus.

Click on the **draw table** icon.

.: Draw box size :.

Draw the first box the size you want the table. Then draw in the number of rows and columns. You can make them any width you need them to be. When you have finished drawing your table, click the **draw table** symbol again to turn it off. You can now add text to the table as before.

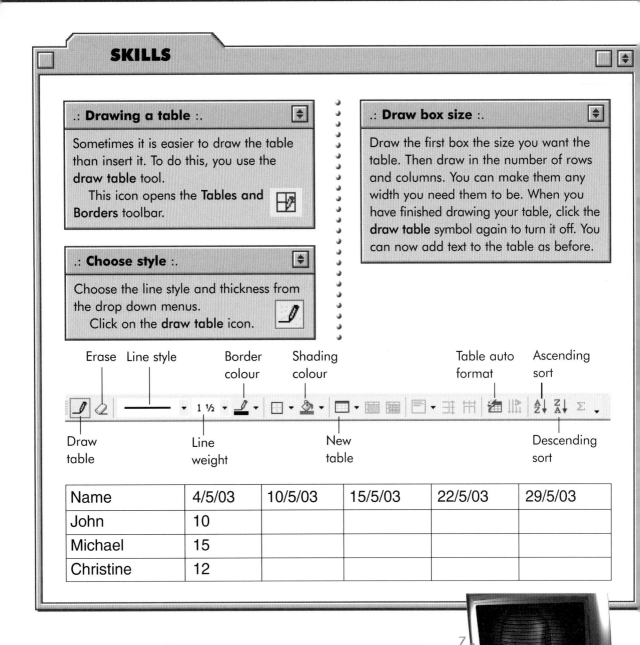

Name	4/5/03	10/5/03	15/5/03	22/5/03	29/5/03
John	10				
Michael	15				
Christine	12				

💡 PC MASTER TIP

You can turn off the drawing pen by pressing **Enter** on the keyboard.

PROGRESS CHECK EXERCISE

Can you make a calendar using the Table menu?

1. Open a new page in Word. Draw a table with eight rows and four columns using the Table toolbar.

2. Put a double line border round the edge and a thick single line to divide up the boxes.

3. Enter the days of the week down the side. At the top of the three remaining columns, put Morning, Afternoon and Evening.

4. Now fill in the chart to show what you are doing next week.

Days of the week	Morning	Afternoon	Evening
Monday			Cinema
Tuesday			
Wednesday	Shopping		Keep fit
Thursday			
Friday			Out for meal
Saturday	London	London	London
Sunday	London	London	London

5. Save your work and print it.

6. Select the table. Copy and paste it below the existing table ready for next week.

✔ MASTERCLASS

To make your calendar clearer, you need to colour the different boxes to show which are work items and which are personal. Colour all the personal items yellow and the work items light blue. Click in the box and then click on the down arrow next to the paint pot. Choose the colour you want.

0100101010110100101001011101001010101011010101101100001010

SKILLS

.: Tables :.

Tables are extremely useful in documents. They help organise information and set out work in a clear way. When you are using a table in a document, you can make changes to the number of rows and columns. You can sort information, change the colours of the cells and make columns different widths. This is called formatting and editing the table. It saves time because you do not have to start from scratch if you need to change what you did originally.

.: Inserting rows and columns :.

First insert a table on to the page. Then type the text into the table.

If you need to add additional rows, select a row. Click on the **tables** button on the toolbar and select **Insert Row Below**.

.: Deleting rows and columns :.

If you want to delete a row, select the row and then click on the **Delete A Row** button. ⥱

To insert or delete a column, you need to select the column and then click on the relevant button in the toolbar menu.

.: Changing column widths :.

Move the mouse pointer over the lines in the table. The mouse pointer will change to two lines and some side arrows.

Click the left mouse button and hold it down while you drag the line to the position you want. You can do the same with rows or columns.

PC MASTER TIP

If you are doing a lot of work with a table, switch on the Tables and Borders menu by selecting the **tables** button on the toolbar. If not, you will need to use the **Table** drop down menu from the main menu bar.

010010010110100101010101011101001010101011101010110111000010101

SKILL IN ACTION

Sue the Scientist often uses tables to present scientific information in reports and publications. She wants the tables to look their best so that the information is easy to read. Recently she has done a report for a health magazine on how much energy you use when exercising.

Activity	Kilocalories (per min approx)	Kilocalories (per hour)
Swimming	10	600
Cycling	6	360
Walking	4	240
Total calories used in exercise for 3 hours a day		1200

EXERCISE

I am collecting data on planets. Draw a table like the one below and fill in the information. Adjust the size of the columns to fit the data. When you have finished, add Neptune to the table. Insert a row for it and complete the data.

Planet	Distance from the sun	Diameter
Jupiter		
Earth		
Venus		
Saturn		
Uranus		
Mercury		
Mars		
Pluto		

SKILLS

.: Adding colour and shading :.

Select the cell or row you want to colour from the **Tables and Borders** toolbar. Click on the down arrow next to the **fill** button. Select the colour you want and the highlighted rows will be coloured.

Fill icon

Monday	Tuesday	Wednesday	Thursday	Friday
			Meeting	
Finish report				
	Meal out	Dentist		Weekend starts

.: To add additional rows :.

First select a row by highlighting it. Go to **Table** on the menu bar, select **Insert** and then choose if you want to add the row above or below.

Table	Window	Help		
Insert	▶		Table...	
Delete	▶	⊔	Columns to the Right	
Merge Cells		⊐⊑	Rows Above	
AutoFit	▶	⊐⊑	Rows Below	
Formula...			⌄	

.: Merging cells :.

To merge cells, highlight the cells you want to join together. Then click on the **merge** button from the toolbar.

Merge icon

Monday	Tuesday	Wednesday	Thursday	Friday
			Meeting	
Finish report		Dentist		
	Meal out			Weekend starts

Sort

Sort by
Column 1 ▼ Type: Text ▼ ● Ascending ○ Descending
Using: Paragraphs ▼

Then by
▼ Type: Text ▼ ● Ascending ○ Descending
Using: Paragraphs ▼

Then by
▼ Type: Text ▼ ○ Ascending ○ Descending
Using: Paragraphs ▼

My list has
○ Header row   ● No header row

Options...   OK   Cancel

PC MASTER TIP

You can sort the information in a table by ascending or descending order. When sorting, 'ascending' is smallest to largest, 'descending' is largest to smallest.

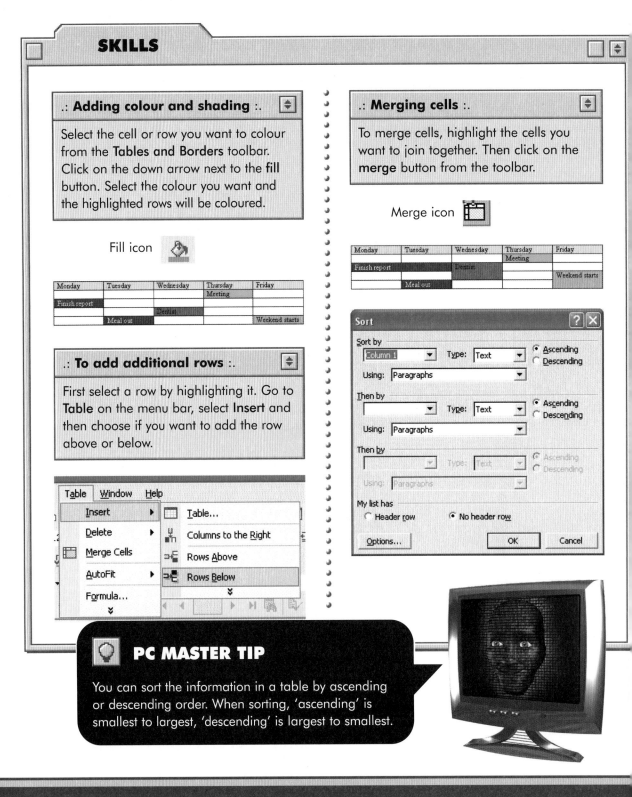

001001010101101001010010111010010101010111010101101110000101

PROGRESS CHECK EXERCISE

Can you open a Word document and draw a table containing three columns and seven rows?

1. Make one row into a heading by merging cells.

2. Format the heading font and colour.

3. Put headings on the other columns as seen in the picture below.

4. Add the following information to the table. Can you move between the cells in the table using the tab button?

5. Now add five additional rows.

6. Add more information of your own to complete the table.

7. Save your work.

8. Sort the table by date in ascending order.

Music collection		
Title	**Artist**	**Purchased**
The Beatles 1	The Beatles	12/03/96
Power of Ten	Chris De Burgh	30/05/00
The Essential	Simon and Garfunkel	26/10/99
Small World Big Band	Jools Holland	12/12/01
Lazy	David Bryne	11/12/02

 MASTERCLASS

Create a birthday chart for your family so you can display it on the wall. You need to use colour and shading in the cells to highlight key dates, for example family in one colour and friends in another. Sort the table by date. Put borders on your table. Put a different border around the outside of the table from the lines in the middle.

010010101101001010010101101001010101011101010110110001010

SKILLS

.: Header and footer uses :.

Headers and footers are areas in the top and bottom margins of each page in a document. They give information to the reader, for example the date the document was created or the author of the document.

You can insert text or graphics in headers and footers, for example page numbers, a company logo, or the document's title or file name. This is useful if you want to find the document on your computer and edit it.

.: Adding headers and footers :.

On the **View** menu, click **Header and Footer** to open the header or footer area on a page.

To create a header, enter text or graphics in the header area.

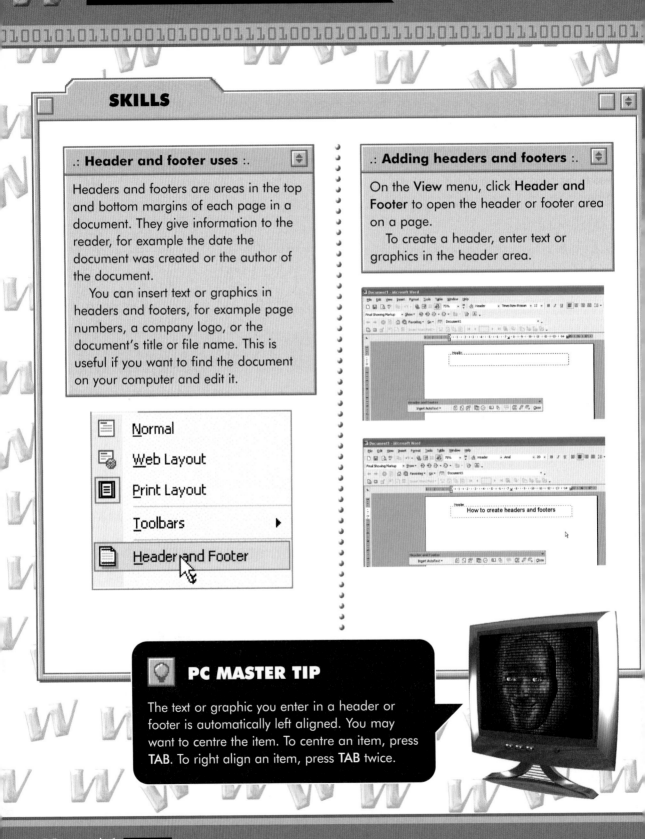

	Normal
	Web Layout
	Print Layout
	Toolbars ▶
	Header and Footer

💡 PC MASTER TIP

The text or graphic you enter in a header or footer is automatically left aligned. You may want to centre the item. To centre an item, press **TAB**. To right align an item, press **TAB** twice.

0010010101011010010101010101110100101010101011101010101101101100001010

SKILL IN ACTION

Max the Marketing Executive always uses the headers and footers on his documents to promote the corporate image.

Black and white marketing company

This header image will appear on all the pages in this document

He saves his header as a template by going to File, Save As.

In the File name: box he puts 'corporate image' and in the Save in: box – document 'Templates'. Then he clicks on Save.

To use the template – when he goes to File, New he chooses 'General' from the templates task pane and selects the one he wants.

EXERCISE

Using Word, write a short report on a film you have seen recently. Put a header on the document showing a character from the film.

SKILLS

.: Switching header and footer :.

Open the **header and footer** toolbar from the **View** menu. To create a footer, click **Switch between Header and Footer** on the toolbar to move to the footer area. Then enter text or graphics.

When you have finished, click **Close** on the header and footer toolbar.

.: Switching header and footer :.

You can insert a field into a footer by using **AutoText**.

Select what you want to appear in the footer. It will automatically be attached to all the pages in the document.

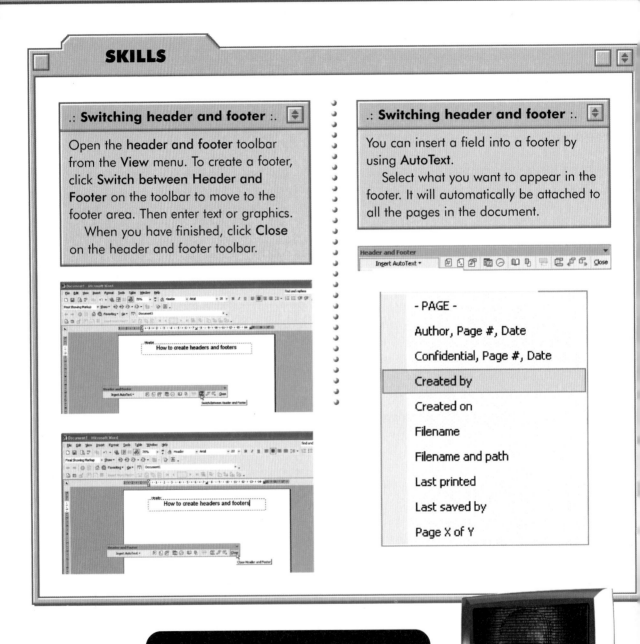

- PAGE -

Author, Page #, Date

Confidential, Page #, Date

Created by

Created on

Filename

Filename and path

Last printed

Last saved by

Page X of Y

PC MASTER TIP

You can also use buttons on the **Header and Footer** toolbar to enter text into the header and footer area.

001001010101101001010010101110100101010101110101010110111000010101

PROGRESS CHECK EXERCISE

Can you create a template for a travel company?

1. Open a Word document.
2. Insert a header on to the page that contains a logo or image.
3. Add text to the header.
4. Add a footer to the template. This should include the date, author and file name.

2. Add the company address and date on the right.
3. Write the letter.
4. Change the information in the footer.
5. Save your work and print it.

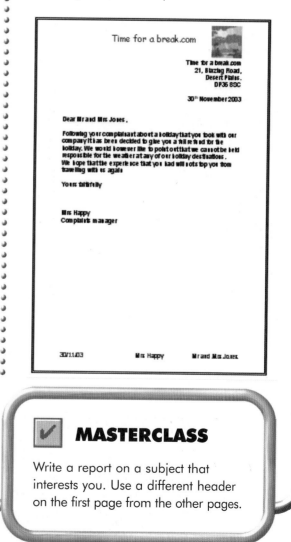

Can you write a letter to a customer who has just returned from a nightmare holiday, which the travel company organised for them?

1. Open the template you have created.

✓ MASTERCLASS

Write a report on a subject that interests you. Use a different header on the first page from the other pages.

SKILLS

.: Creating text boxes :.

Text boxes and frames are both containers for text. You can position and size them on a page.

On the **Drawing** toolbar, click the **text box** icon. Drag out a box to the size you want. When you insert a text box, a drawing canvas appears around it, but you can drag the text box off the canvas if you want to.

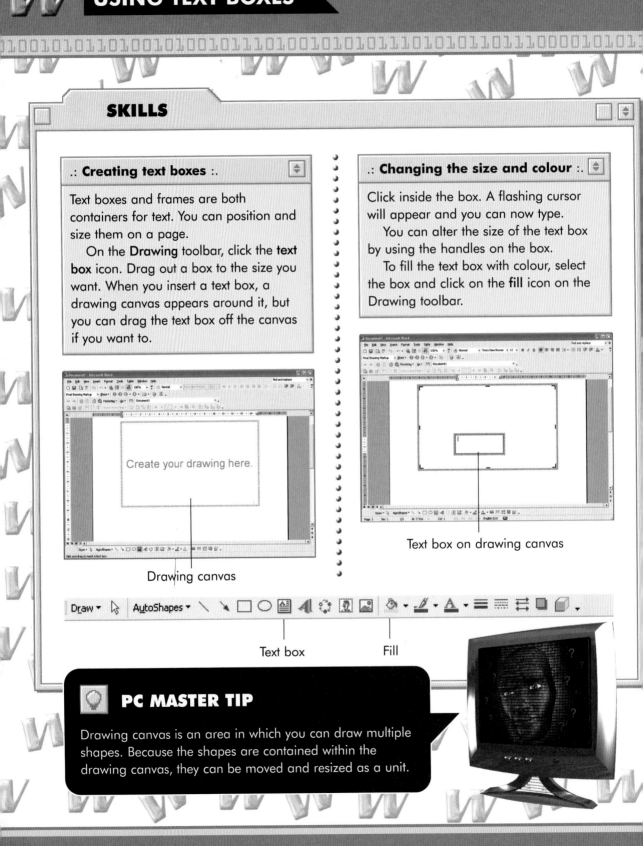

Create your drawing here.

Drawing canvas

.: Changing the size and colour :.

Click inside the box. A flashing cursor will appear and you can now type.

You can alter the size of the text box by using the handles on the box.

To fill the text box with colour, select the box and click on the **fill** icon on the Drawing toolbar.

Text box on drawing canvas

Text box   Fill

💡 PC MASTER TIP

Drawing canvas is an area in which you can draw multiple shapes. Because the shapes are contained within the drawing canvas, they can be moved and resized as a unit.

SKILL IN ACTION

Tammy the Teacher uses text boxes when she is preparing interactive activities for her class. She first inserts an image of a flower on to the page. Then she puts the labels in text boxes. In the lesson, she asks the students to move the words to the correct part of the plant. Then they add additional information to the boxes, explaining the function of each part of the plant. They resize the boxes. When they are happy with the labelled picture, they print it out.

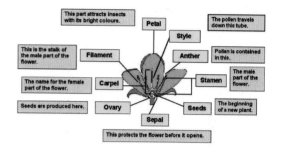

EXERCISE

I am preparing an activity for an English lesson on story beginnings. Can you type each sentence into a different text box and muddle them up? My class can then move them around so that the story makes sense.

Story Starts

This morning, his eyes went straight to it - and stared.

But the best thing was the huge crane that towered over his school, where the new buildings were going up.

The car reached the top of the hill and Ben leaned forward to see the town ahead, spread out in the valley.

He loved spotting the church spires and the shops and the park.

'What's that?' he whispered. 'That silver thing hanging from the crane? It looks like - but that's impossible!'

The crane had -

SKILLS

.: **Formatting a text box** :.

By formatting the text box you can add 3-D effects, shadows, border styles and colours, fills, and backgrounds. You can also change the orientation of the text in a text box by using the **text direction** icon.

First, add the text box to the page.

Make sure the text box is selected by clicking once inside the box with the left mouse button.

Right click and select **Format Text Box** from the menu.

.: **Changing the appearance** :.

A window will appear. Select the fill colour or border you want and click **OK**.

If you want to add other effects, select the buttons from the Drawing toolbar.

.: **Changing the appearance** :.

To change the shape of the text box, select the box. Go to **Draw** on the toolbar and click on **Change AutoShape**. Choose the style from the options.

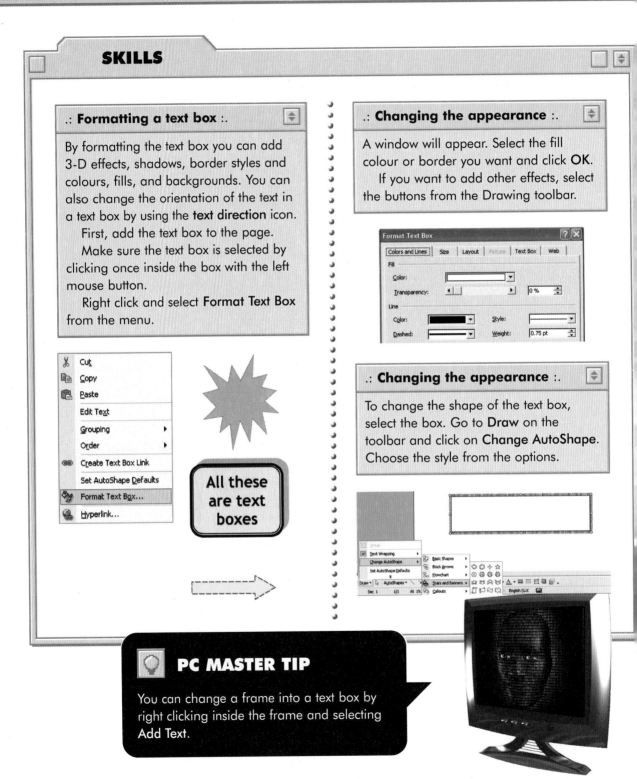

All these are text boxes

PC MASTER TIP

You can change a frame into a text box by right clicking inside the frame and selecting **Add Text**.

0010010101011010010100101011101001010101011101010101110111000010010

PROGRESS CHECK EXERCISE

Can you create a poster for people new to your school or place of work about how your school or company deals with bullying?

1. Open a Word document.

2. Insert your images: clipart, photos or pictures from the internet.

3. Arrange them on the page using the Format Picture toolbar.

4. Add text boxes with relevant text. Choose the colour, shape and style of the text boxes to create maximum impact.

5. Save your work.

6. Add a border to your poster.

7. Print your work.

 MASTERCLASS

Use text boxes to create an information sheet about how to use a feature in Word that you have found useful. To create images for your sheet, you will need to take screenshots by pressing **PRT SC** on your keyboard. Then go into Word and paste them. Once the image is in Word, you can edit it.

USING WORD ART

SKILLS

.: Word art style :.

Word art can be used to create impact and interest to a page.

To create word art click on the **Insert** menu. Click **Picture** and select **WordArt**.

A window will open. Select the style of word art you want and click **OK**.

.: Enter text :.

A different view of the window will open and you can now enter the text.

Click on **OK** and the text will be entered on the page as an image.

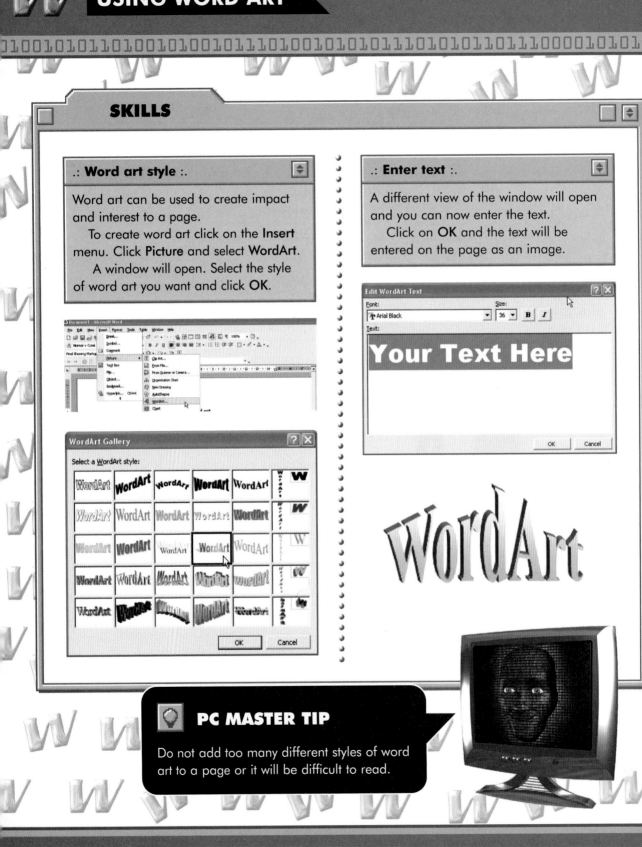

PC MASTER TIP

Do not add too many different styles of word art to a page or it will be difficult to read.

SKILL IN ACTION

Vicrum the Vet uses word art to attract attention to important notices in his surgery or on leaflets he sends out to his clients. To save time, he often reuses previously saved work and edits the text.

Vicrum can then change the look of the poster by using the Editing toolbar.

EXERCISE

I am planning to run some new dog training classes and want to advertise them in the surgery. Can you create a poster using WordArt to attract people's attention? The poster should contain a picture, dates, times and cost of the classes.

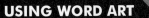

SKILLS

.: WordArt toolbar :.

Open a document from **File** that contains word art. Select the word art by single clicking with the left mouse button. This opens the **WordArt** toolbar.

.: Edit text :.

From the menu select **Edit Text**. A window opens and you will see the present text. Delete this text and enter the new text. When you are happy, click **OK**. The old text is replaced by the new text.

.: Changing colours and fonts :.

Sometimes the WordArt templates that you choose are the wrong colour and font for your design. You can change these using the WordArt toolbar.

PC MASTER TIP

Using the toolbar, you can change the layout of the picture. You can position it anywhere on the page by clicking on the **text-wrapping** icon. To find this, move the mouse slowly over the icons and a pop-up text will tell you what each one is for.

PROGRESS CHECK EXERCISE

Can you create an invitation for a party?

Include word art and images. Remember to put in the date, the time and the venue.

MASTERCLASS

Create an original design for labels using WordArt. You will need to change the colour, font and size of the original template. You can do this by using the Edit toolbar.

SKILLS

.: Using hyperlinks :.

Hyperlinks are very useful when you want to link to another document on your computer or to a website. If you have a large document or project, you can link the contents page to the correct chapter so you do not have to look through the whole document. An example of this is **Help** files in Microsoft® Word.

.: Using hyperlinks :.

First of all, right click on the page. Select **Hyperlink** from the pop-up menu.

.: Using hyperlinks :.

A window will open. Type the text you want to display for your link in the top box. From the left-hand menu select the first option: **Existing File or Webpage**.
     Select the file from the window in the centre. Click **OK**. The link will appear on the page with a blue underline. This shows it is a link. When you click it, it will take you to the document you have selected.

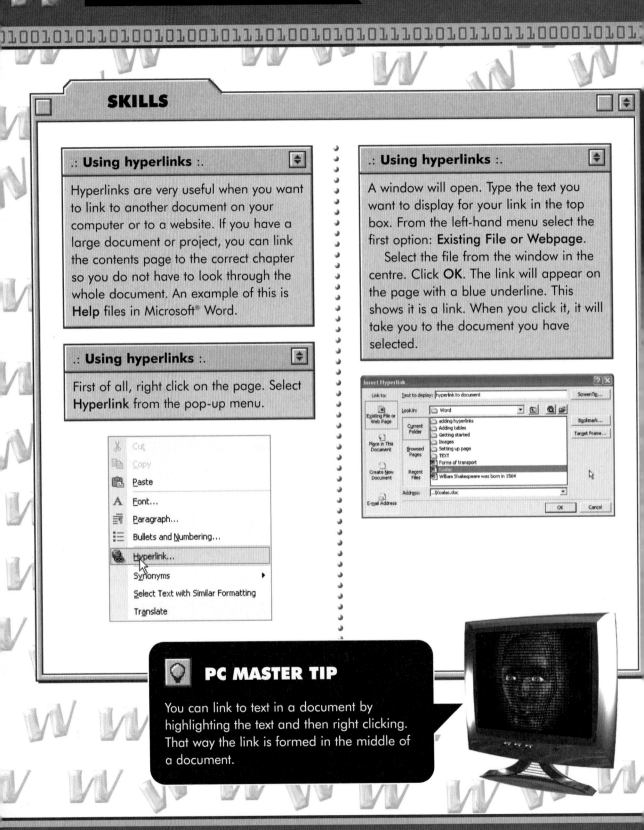

PC MASTER TIP

You can link to text in a document by highlighting the text and then right clicking. That way the link is formed in the middle of a document.

`0010010101101001010010110100101010110101011011100001010`

SKILL IN ACTION

Tammy the Teacher is planning for her class to do a geography project about tourism. To support this work she wants the pupils to investigate holiday resorts around the United Kingdom. To help them with this work she provides them with a page of hyperlinks to take them to good websites where they can collect reliable and relevant information.

She explains to the students that this is something travel agents might use for their customers if they want to find out information about the holiday destination of their choice.

Tourism

www.world-tourism.org – a useful site which gives you lots of general information.

www.englishtourism.org.uk – this site is the new Visit Britain site which has been set up recently to market tourism in Britain.

www.travelengland.org.uk - a good site for exploring places to visit and stay. Clear easy to follow information.

www.somerset.gov.uk/tourism - this site is focused on one particular area of the UK. These sorts of sites are available for lots of different areas. Some additional areas are below.
www.cheshire.gov.uk/tourism/home.htm
www.pooletourism.com

www.tourism.wales.gov.uk – the main Welsh tourist board.

www.greentourism.org.uk – this site focuses on the environmental aspect of tourism in Scotland.

EXERCISE

I am creating a handbook for the school. I have a number of items on the contents page and want you to link these to the relevant documents.

Contents page
School day times
Holiday dates
Blank timetable

First, create the documents using text and tables and save them to **My Documents** under the headings above. Then create a contents page and hyperlinks to the correct documents.

> Contents page
>
> School day times
> Holiday dates
> Blank timetable

SKILLS

.: Link to a web page :.

To link to a web page, right click on the page. Select **Hyperlink** as before and the window will appear. This time, click on the 🔍 . This will launch your internet browser. Search for the internet page you want and its address will appear in the address box at the bottom of the page. Make sure the text you want to display is correct and click **OK**. If you do not add text to be displayed, the web page heading will be the text.

.: Link to a web page :.

To link to a picture, click on the image with the right mouse button. Select **Hyperlink** from the menu and link to a website as before. When you put your mouse over the picture, the computer will tell you how to follow the link.

You can also link to other parts of the same document. This is very useful if you have a long document or if you are working on web pages.

CTRL + click to follow link

News

PC MASTER TIP

To check the hyperlinks work, hold down the **control** key and click on the link at the same time. This will open the web page or document you have linked to.

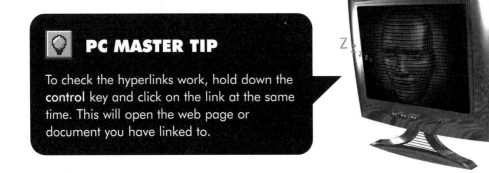

PROGRESS CHECK EXERCISE

Can you open a page in Microsoft® Word and write a short report about a topical news item?

1. Put an image on your page about your news item.

No smoking in public

Doctors have called for an outright ban on smoking in public.

The doctors, from the Royal College of Physicians and 17 other medical colleges have said they now strongly believe evidence about the dangers of passive smoking.

It is not the first time the question has been raised. Those against a ban say it is the government infringing on our freedom of choice. Many publicans claim it will be bad for business.

The doctors however say that 1,000 adults are killed each year by breathing in other people's smoke. There is also evidence that it causes asthma, lung infections, and ear problems in children.

In an open letter to a newspaper, the doctors argue that voluntary no smoking policies are not working. Now, bars and pubs can choose whether to ban smoking and, as a result, only 36 pubs in the whole country have done so.

Restaurants have been slightly more health conscious and one restaurant chain is banning smoking altogether for its customers.

2. Add a hyperlink from your news item to a website with more information about the story.

No smoking in public

Doctors have called for an outright ban on smoking in public.

The doctors, from the Royal College of Physicians and 17 other medical colleges have said they now strongly believe evidence about the dangers of passive smoking.

It is not the first time the question has been raised. Those against a ban say it is the government infringing on our freedom of choice. Many publicans claim it will be bad for business.

The doctors however say that 1,000 adults are killed each year by breathing in other people's smoke. There is also evidence that it causes asthma, lung infections, and ear problems in children.

In an open letter to a newspaper, the doctors argue that voluntary no smoking policies are not working. Now, bars and pubs can choose whether to ban smoking and, as a result, only 36 pubs in the whole country have done so.

Restaurants have been slightly more health conscious and one restaurant chain is banning smoking altogether for its customers.

For further information click here

3. Create a second page containing further information and images on your news story.

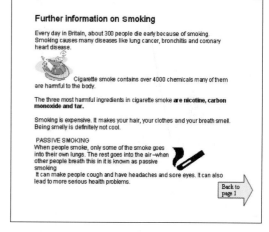

Further information on smoking

Every day in Britain, about 300 people die early because of smoking. Smoking causes many diseases like lung cancer, bronchitis and coronary heart disease.

Cigarette smoke contains over 4000 chemicals many of them are harmful to the body.

The three most harmful ingredients in cigarette smoke **are nicotine, carbon monoxide and tar.**

Smoking is expensive. It makes your hair, your clothes and your breath smell. Being smelly is definitely not cool.

PASSIVE SMOKING
When people smoke, only some of the smoke goes into their own lungs. The rest goes into the air –when other people breath this in it is known as passive smoking

It can make people cough and have headaches and sore eyes. It can also lead to more serious health problems.

Back to page 1

Can you hyperlink the image on your first page to the second page containing further pictures related to the story?

Now put a link back to the original page.

✔ MASTERCLASS

Prepare an information sheet that contains several sections. At the beginning of your document, include a contents page. Hyperlink the index to the relevant sections in the document.

SKILLS

.: Inserting sound from clipart :.

Adding a sound to a document can be very useful when it it difficult to explain something in words or to add more detail and interest. Sound is only effective if the document is viewed on the computer.

To make use of sound you will need to have speakers attached to your computer.

Select **Insert** from the menu bar and select **Picture From Clipart**. When the **Insert Clipart** window opens, select from the **Results should be:** box and click on the down arrow. Make sure the sound box is the only box ticked.

.: Sound symbol :.

In the **Search text:** box enter the type of sound you are looking for, for example animals. Then click **Search**.

When the list of sounds appears decide which one you want and click **Insert** and a sound symbol will be inserted.

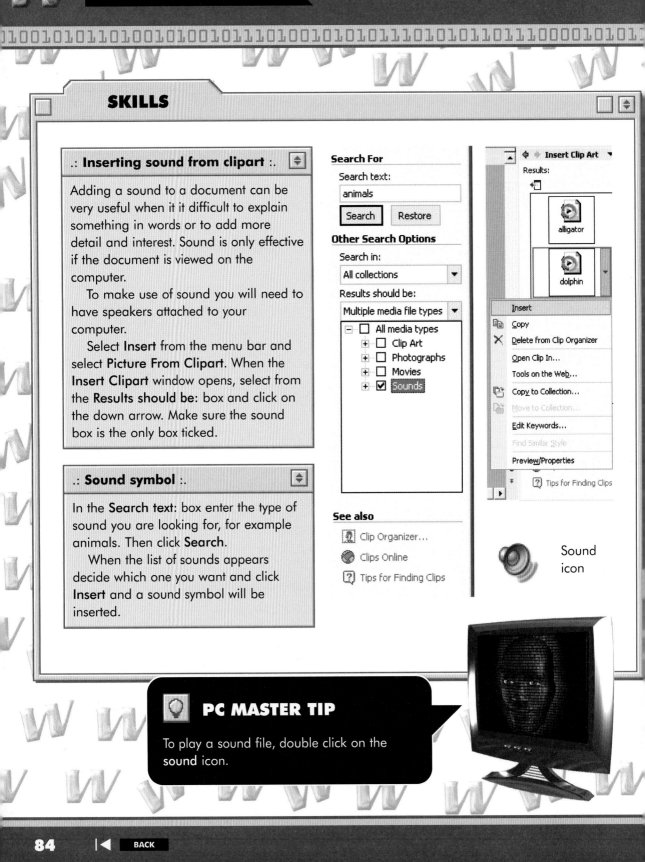

Search For

Search text:

animals

Search   Restore

Other Search Options

Search in:

All collections   ▼

Results should be:

Multiple media file types   ▼

⊟ ☐ All media types
  ⊞ ☐ Clip Art
  ⊞ ☐ Photographs
  ⊞ ☐ Movies
  ⊞ ☑ Sounds

See also

🖼 Clip Organizer...
⊙ Clips Online
❓ Tips for Finding Clips

◆ ◆ Insert Clip Art ▼

Results:

alligator

dolphin

Insert
Copy
Delete from Clip Organizer
Open Clip In...
Tools on the Web...
Copy to Collection...
Move to Collection...
Edit Keywords...
Find Similar Style
Preview/Properties

❓ Tips for Finding Clips

Sound icon

💡 PC MASTER TIP

To play a sound file, double click on the **sound** icon.

SKILL IN ACTION

Kate the Kitchen Designer adds sound files to the presentations she does for clients. She also records details of the clients' requirements and attaches them to her records. Sound files added to the presentations give extra details when she shows her clients the designs. Kate saves her files as web pages for the clients to view.

She chooses a blank page from the menu when she opens a document and then adds images and text to the page. She changes the background of the document for effect and then adds a sound file to the document. Finally, she saves the file as a web page and previews it using Web Page Preview from the File menu.

Suggested kitchen design

Layout - shows ease of movement and the three major appliances within easy reach.

Two alternative colour schemes based on the clients' preferences.

Suggested furniture styles.

EXERCISE

Can you prepare a presentation for the design of a room in your house as a web page in Word? Add images, text, and sound to your presentation. Use music and narration to help give extra information and effect. Preview your page as a web page and listen to the sound.

100101011010010100101110100101010110101011011000010101

SKILLS

.: Recording sound :.

To record sound you will need to have a microphone connected to your PC and either headphones or speakers to listen to the sounds.

From the **Insert** menu, select **Object**. When the window opens, select **Create New** and then **Wave Sound**. The sound recorder window will open. Click on the red **record** button [●] and begin your narration. It is always a good idea to plan what you want to say before you start. When you have finished click on the **stop** button [■].

Sound recorder window

Stop
Record

.: Listen to the sound :.

When you have finished close the sound recorder window and return to the document you were writing.

The **sound** icon will be on the page. Double click on the icon to listen to the sound. To move the icon to a different place on the page, right click, select **Format Object** and then **Layout**. Choose **In front of text** to move the icon freely on the page.

Object

Create New | Create from File

Object type:
TX - ButtonBar Control
TX - Ruler Control
TX - StatusBar Control
TX - Text Control
Ulead COOL 360 Viewer Document
Video Clip
Wave Sound
Windows Media Player

☐ Display as icon

Result

Inserts a new Wave Sound object into your document.

OK | Cancel

.: Link a picture to a sound :.

Insert a picture on the page. Select the picture and right click over the picture. From the menu select **Hyperlink**. Browse to the file you want to add. Click **OK** and the picture will now play the sound when you **Ctrl** click on it. You know if the image is hyperlinked because the mouse pointer changes to a hand symbol.

💡 PC MASTER TIP

You can link to saved files if you create your sound files by using **Sound Recorder** before you start your document. In Sound Recorder you can add effects to your sounds like an echo.

PROGRESS CHECK EXERCISE

Can you write an article for an electronic magazine about an environmental issue, for example Global Warming?

1. Your article needs to be accessible for partially sighted people. You need to include narration of the text as a sound file and, as the number of written words is limited to 100 because of space on the page, you need to add additional information through sound recordings.

2. Open a Word document and write your article. Add suitable images to the page.

3. Record the text as a narration and add it to the page as a sound file.

4. Now use Sound Recorder, Music, and Sound Effects to add additional information and effects to the article.

5. Save your work.

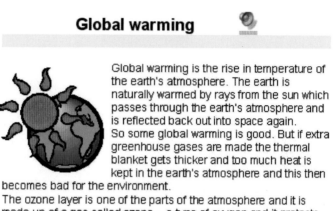

Global warming

Global warming is the rise in temperature of the earth's atmosphere. The earth is naturally warmed by rays from the sun which passes through the earth's atmosphere and is reflected back out into space again.
So some global warming is good. But if extra greenhouse gases are made the thermal blanket gets thicker and too much heat is kept in the earth's atmosphere and this then becomes bad for the environment.
The ozone layer is one of the parts of the atmosphere and it is made up of a gas called ozone – a type of oxygen and it protects the earth from harmful rays.

✓ MASTERCLASS

Create a report of a visit or holiday you have been on. Add a sound explanation to your report. Position the sound icon on the page so it is easy to see.

SKILLS

.: Drawing tools :.

Images can add interest to a page and emphasise key points. In this section we will be finding out how to draw our own images.

You can display the **Drawing** toolbar by clicking on the **drawing** icon on the standard toolbar.

Click it again and the toolbar disappears. This is known as a **toggle** icon.

.: Basic shapes :.

To draw a basic shape, click once with the left mouse button on the rectangle or oval shaped icon. Move the mouse pointer on to your page and it will change to a cross hair $+$. Wherever you click on the page will now be the top left hand corner of your shape. Hold the left mouse button down and drag the rectangle to the size you want.

.: Adding colour :.

Select the shape by clicking anywhere on the border. You can now change the line thickness and add colour to the shapes by clicking on the **line style** tool and the **fill** tool.

If you click the border, you will be able to move the shape. If you want to change the shape, you need to drag one of the handles.

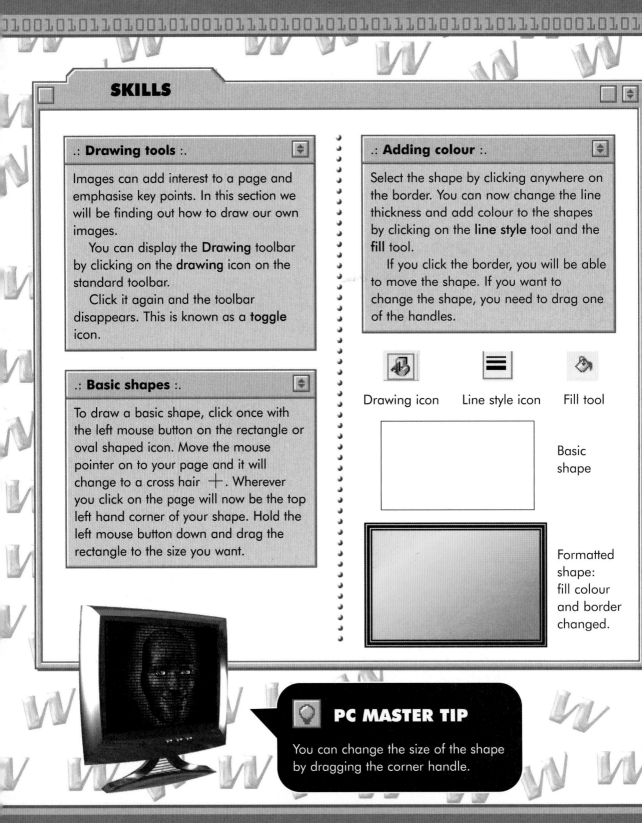

Drawing icon   Line style icon   Fill tool

Basic shape

Formatted shape: fill colour and border changed.

PC MASTER TIP

You can change the size of the shape by dragging the corner handle.

SKILL IN ACTION

Harry the Hotelier has recently been advertising his Christmas promotions in the local newspaper, on posters and leaflets. In all his advertising he has used drawings to add impact to his advertising materials.

Harry is very careful not to use too many different colours on adverts as this can make the product look messy. He chooses carefully where he wants the emphasis to be on the page as the shapes and colours draw the eye to that place.

Christmas
Murder Mystery Nights

Join us for a great night of festive fun, good food and a great atmosphere. Party with our resident DJ until 1a.m.

5th & 17th December

The White Swan Hotel
Mere Street,
Claverdon

£25 per person

EXERCISE

Can you design and make a poster advertising the new health spa opening at Harry's hotel? Decorate it with suitable shapes and images which reflect the health spa's image.

1100101011010010100101011010010101011101010101101110000101011

SKILLS

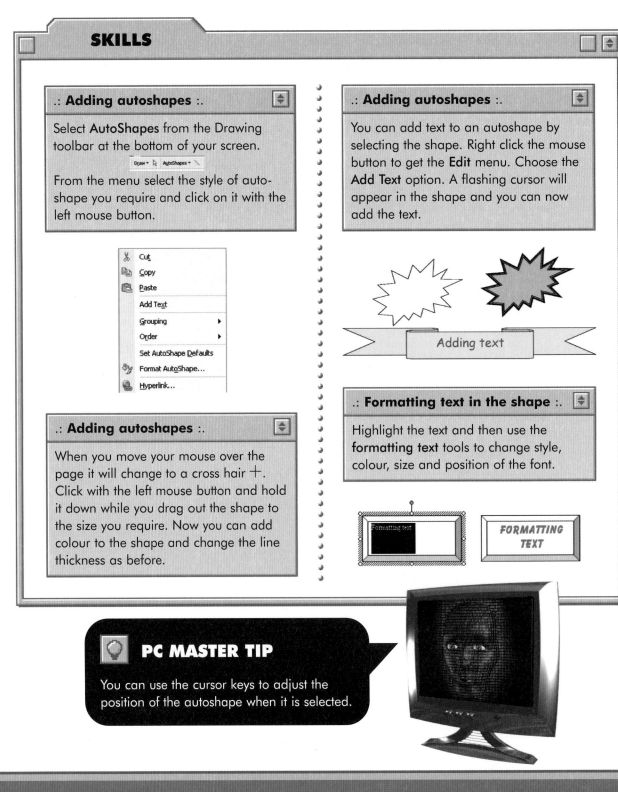

.: Adding autoshapes :.

Select **AutoShapes** from the Drawing toolbar at the bottom of your screen.

Draw ▾ | ⌖ | AutoShapes ▾ | ╲

From the menu select the style of auto-shape you require and click on it with the left mouse button.

.: Adding autoshapes :.

You can add text to an autoshape by selecting the shape. Right click the mouse button to get the **Edit** menu. Choose the **Add Text** option. A flashing cursor will appear in the shape and you can now add the text.

✄	Cu_t
🗐	_C_opy
📋	_P_aste
	Add Te_x_t
	_G_rouping ▸
	O_r_der ▸
	Set AutoShape _D_efaults
✐	Format Aut_o_Shape...
🔗	_H_yperlink...

Adding text

.: Formatting text in the shape :.

Highlight the text and then use the **formatting text** tools to change style, colour, size and position of the font.

.: Adding autoshapes :.

When you move your mouse over the page it will change to a cross hair +. Click with the left mouse button and hold it down while you drag out the shape to the size you require. Now you can add colour to the shape and change the line thickness as before.

Formatting text

FORMATTING TEXT

💡 PC MASTER TIP

You can use the cursor keys to adjust the position of the autoshape when it is selected.

PROGRESS CHECK EXERCISE

Can you open a Word document and insert five different autoshapes on the page?

Move the shapes on the page and resize them so they fill the page.

Fill each shape with a different colour. Change the line colour, style and thickness on each shape.

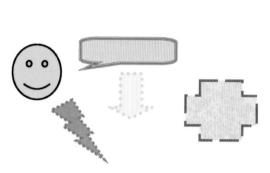

Can you now add text to one of the boxes, then change the font style and colour?

These shapes were created using AutoShapes.

✓ MASTERCLASS

Create a three-fold leaflet to promote a local business. Before you begin, look at some of the business's literature to identify the key features of their corporate image.

MAIL MERGE

SKILLS

.: Mail merge wizard :.

Mail merging allows you to personalise a standard letter. Rather than having to alter a letter for each person, you can write one letter which Word will automatically duplicate. Word puts individual personal information into the appropriate places. You can also use the mail merge tool to address envelopes, create mailing labels or to produce personalised documents.

Click on the **File** menu and choose **New Blank Document**. Then click on the **Tools** menu and choose **Letters and Mailing**, then **Mail Merge Wizard**.

The mail merge wizard will appear down the right-hand side of the screen.

Select document type

What type of document
are you working on?

- ● Letters
- ○ E-mail messages
- ○ Envelopes
- ○ Labels
- ○ Directory

Letters

Send letters to a group of
people. You can
personalize the letter that
each person receives.

.: Create a letter :.

Choose **Letters** from the wizard menu. Click on the blue coloured link at the bottom of the Wizard Menu.

➡ Next: Starting document

On the next screen, select **use current document** then move to Step 3 of 6 by clicking on the link **Select recipients**.

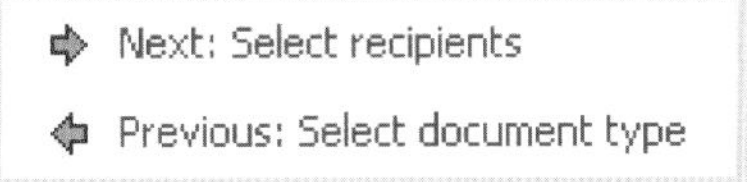

➡ Next: Select recipients

⬅ Previous: Select document type

Choose **Type a new list** and then click on **Create**. A window will open to allow you to fill in names and addresses of the recipients for the letter.

Move to the next step – write the letter then add the address and greetings as instructed in the wizard.

Move to step 5 of 6 and preview the letter. Make any changes at this stage. When you are satisfied, move to the final stage, and **Complete the merge**.

PC MASTER TIP

You can merge documents with people in your Outlook address book so you do not have to type out the address list every time.

SKILL IN ACTION

Vicrum the Vet has been collecting money for an endangered species charity. To save time, he wants to send the same letter out to everybody. To do this, he is using mail merge for the letters and the envelopes.

He uses the addresses in his Outlook contacts rather than having to create a list every time.

Rose Garden Animal Sanctuary
Fragrant Lane
Summerfield

05 December 2004

24, Green Lane
Leamington Spa
CV36 8RD

Dear Mrs Jones,

Thank you for your help and support at the recent fundraising event held at the Animal Sanctuary in aid of endangered species.
I am please to tell you that we raised a total of £576 80p. We are now able to add our total to the rest of the fundraising events held in our area to bring it to a grand total of £2010.

Thank you again for your support and I look forward to working with you next time we support such a worthy cause.

Yours truly,

Rose Garden Animal Sanctuary
Fragrant Lane
Summerfield

05 December 2004

85, White Street
Leamington Spa
CV37 4FL

Dear Mr French,

Thank you for your help and support at the recent fundraising event held at the Animal Sanctuary in aid of endangered species.
I am please to tell you that we raised a total of £576 80p. We are now able to add our total to the rest of the fundraising events held in our area to bring it to a grand total of £2010.

Thank you again for your support and I look forward to working with you next time we support such a worthy cause.

Yours truly,

EXERCISE

Write a letter giving all the information: dates, times, venue and purpose of a bring and buy sale.

Open the mail merge wizard and follow the instructions. When it asks you to select recipients click on **Type a new list**. Put four names and addresses into your list. Complete the mail merge by following the wizard.

Save your work and print out four letters.

01001010101101001010010101101001010101101010110110101100001010101

SKILLS

.: Merge link :.

Click on the **File** menu and choose **New Blank Document**. Then click on the **Tools** menu and choose **Mail Merge**. The mail merge wizard will appear down the right-hand side of the screen.

Choose **Letter** from the wizard menu. Click on the link-starting document at the bottom of the page.

Select **Present Document** from the second menu.

Go to the next page. Click on **Select from Outlook contacts**. Browse for the contact folder you want to use in Outlook. Select the mail recipients and then click **OK**.

If you do not have any contacts in Outlook, click on **Type a new list** and add the names and addresses of the people you want to send the letters to.

Click on the next step in the wizard and follow the instructions as before.

Click on **Complete Merge Link** and then send the items to the printer.

Select recipients

- ○ Use an existing list
- ● Select from Outlook contac
- ○ Type a new list

Select from Outlook contacts

Currently, your recipients are selected from:

[Contacts] in "Personal Folders

▦ Choose Contacts Fold

✍ Edit recipient list...

Step 3 of 6

➡ Next: Arrange your labels

⬅ Previous: Starting docume

Mail Merge Recipients ? ✕

To sort the list, click the appropriate column heading. To narrow down the recipients displayed by a specific criteria, such as by city, click the arrow next to the column heading. Use the check boxes or buttons to add or remove recipients from the mail merge.

List of recipients:

	Last Name	First Name	Title	Company Name	Address Line
☑	Brown	Jane	Mrs		
☑	White	Jo	Mr		
☑	Red	Sue	Miss		
☑	Redwood	Fed	Mr		
☑	Greentree	Colin	Mr		
☑	Baker	Lynda	Mrs		

Select All   Clear All   Refresh

Find...   Edit...   Validate   OK

💡 PC MASTER TIP

You can use mail merge to make labels for envelopes. Use the wizard or the Mail Merge toolbar from the Tools menu.

PROGRESS CHECK EXERCISE

Can you make an invitation for a Hallowe'en party? Use clipart, WordArt and different fonts.

Personalise the invitations by using mail merge and adding a greetings line.

MASTERCLASS

Use the mail merge wizard to create address labels and print them out on to a piece of A4 paper.

INDEX

Aligning text 20–23

Backspace 6
Borders 40–43
Bulleting 36–39

Caps 5
  lock 6
ClipArt 44–47
Columns 56–59
Copying 8–11

Delete 6
Drawing 88–91

Enter 6

Find 32–35
Format menu
  picture 52–55

Footers 68–71
Grammar check 28–31

Headers 68–71
Highlighting 34
Hyperlinks 80–83

Images 44–55
Insertion point 16

Mail merge 92–95
Margins 26–27

Numbered lists 36–39

Opening files 12–15
  Word 4–7
Orientation 24–25

Page setup 24–27

Pasting 8–11
Photographs 48–51
Printing 22–23

Replace 32–35
Resizing images
  46–47, 50–51

Saving 12–15
Selecting 16
Shapes 88–91
Shift 5
Sound 84–87
Spellcheck 28–31

Tables 60–67
Text boxes 72–75
  wrapping 52–55

WordArt 76–79